T0130211

An Asperger Journey

My Lifelong Battle with Autism

SCOTT VERBOUT

iUniverse, Inc.
Bloomington

An Asperger Journey
My Lifelong Battle with Autism

iUniverse books may be ordered through booksellers or by contacting:

iUniverse
1663 Liberty Drive
Bloomington, IN 47403
www.iuniverse.com
1-800-Authors (1-800-288-4677)

ISBN: 978-1-4502-9535-2 (pbk)
ISBN: 978-1-4502-9536-9 (ebk)

Printed in the United States of America

iUniverse rev. date: 2/23/11

To my wife and daughter, and everyone who stood
by me as I was going through a difficult time.

INTRODUCTION

Autism is a disorder that is still something of a medical mystery. Although it affects people in various ways, those who have it are believed to process information differently from others in similar situations. Those afflicted often are perceived as being withdrawn from others and being resistant to change, exhibiting narrow interests. According to the Autism Society of America, the condition affects 1 million to 1.5 million people in the United States, and the latest Centers for Disease Control statistics show that 1 in 110 children may be born with this developmental disorder. Until recently, learning those statistics would have meant nothing to me. But that was before I discovered, at age 44, that I suffer from autism.

How did I not know that I had autism before then? It's difficult to explain. Like many people, my initial exposure to autism came from watching Dustin Hoffman's performance in *Rain Man*. Of course, Hoffman portrayed a character with a severe form of autism. I was not aware until a short time ago that there is an autism "spectrum," ranging from very mild to very severe.

And that is just one reason I didn't know I had autism until I was in my 40s: I was totally unaware that such a range of autistic disorders existed. Asperger's syndrome, the type that I have, is one of the mildest forms. It is a high-functioning form of autism, but it is autism just the same. So what exactly is Asperger's syndrome? Behaviors differ; no two autistic people react alike. The Autism Society of America offers this definition: "The essential features of Asperger's Disorder are severe and sustained impairment in social interaction and the development of restricted, repetitive patterns of behavior, interest, and activity." I possess many of these attributes. In addition to being socially awkward, I tend to follow routines, and I have narrow but obsessive interests.

For the most part, I am able to live and work in everyday society. There are times, though, when I feel completely lost in the "normal" world, and I realize how different I am. Because dysfunctional social behavior is one of the key aspects of Asperger's, it's no surprise that those differences seem to crop up most noticeably when I have to deal with other people. My mind thinks one way, whereas "normal" people, known as "neurotypical" in the medical world, think another way.

It is important to note that Asperger's is not just a disorder; it very much can be a disability. Discovering at such a late age that I have Asperger's syndrome has been both a blessing and a curse. I still find it hard to cope in certain situations, but at least now I know what the problem is: Asperger's syndrome. Knowing what the problem is and being able to adjust my behavior are two different things, however. And now that I am older, and fairly set in my ways, I'm finding this disorder harder to deal with. My social awkwardness has gotten me into trouble on any number of occasions, and I'm convinced that it contributed to my losing a job that I'd had for more than 15 years. Unfortunately, I discovered that I had Asperger's too late to save me in that instance. Now that I know about my disorder, I'm trying to get the word out, to explain to others so they can understand. And maybe my story can help someone who has gone through similar difficulties in dealing with Asperger's.

That is why I decided to write this book: to relate several of my experiences in dealing with this disorder and to address some of the problems I've had throughout my life, including depression, that caused me a lot of pain and anguish before I ever knew a condition called Asperger's syndrome existed. By bringing more attention to this disorder, I hope that others who have it will find comfort in knowing that they are not alone. I've also asked my wife and daughter to contribute their experiences to show what it is like to live with someone who has Asperger's. I might not have survived some of the most difficult times if it weren't for the support of my loving family. For people who know someone who may have Asperger's, or any other type of autism, I hope this book will lead to a better understanding of the behavior of those individuals.

CHAPTER ONE:
THE TURNING POINT

I wouldn't write a book about Asperger's syndrome if I didn't think I had a story to tell. For most of us, a defining moment, a turning point in our lives, changes us. For me, that moment came in January 2007 when I was fired from a job I'd held since 1991.

According to my employers, I was fired for sexual harassment. Later in this book, I'll describe the circumstances that led to my dismissal in more detail. However, I was not given many details of the allegations or an opportunity to meet with the employees who made them. After so many years of loyalty to the company, I was left feeling hurt and bitter.

It was my misfortune that, at the time I was fired, I was just beginning to come to grips with Asperger's and the social awkwardness that sometimes plagues me. In fact, my termination came mere weeks after I discovered I possibly had the condition. Knowing about Asperger's has changed my perspective greatly about many things. I wonder now, if I had known about Asperger's earlier, would I have done things a little differently? Would I have recognized behaviors or interactions that could have been misinterpreted as harassment? Would I have insisted on clearing up any misunderstandings? My supervisors were just as clueless when I told them about my condition. It seemed that everyone who was aware of my situation dropped the ball, every step of the way.

Making people aware of Asperger's has become a sort of mission for me. How many other people with Asperger's have gone through a similar kind of humiliating experience? For that matter, how many people out there are unaware that they or a loved one might have Asperger's syndrome?

In my case, my discovery was a fluke. I reasoned that I may have Asperger's after reading a story about autism. Until that moment, no one had ever told me that I might be autistic. At first, it was self-diagnosis, but eventually, I was officially diagnosed by a psychologist. For me, discovering that I had an autistic disorder was a watershed event in my life.

In his diagnosis of me in 2007, the doctor indicated that I am "above average in intelligence" but that I have trouble empathizing with others and have a hampered conversational ability. In addition to Asperger's, I may have social anxiety disorder as well.

The doctor explained how this affected me in the workplace: "What employers may need to understand about Asperger's syndrome is that these individuals are awkward socially and are often good at what they do because they tend to pride themselves on being precise about the things they can do. Others they work with may not understand their behavior."

His diagnosis continued, "[Scott's] social awkwardness may be misunderstood. Unfortunately, others may misinterpret his behavior and not understand that he is simply going through feeling uncomfortable and misunderstanding others himself."

After reading more about Asperger's and thinking back on certain periods of my life, a lot of things began to make sense. Even as a child, I was always a bit different from other kids. I had a tremendous interest in the space program as a youngster, and memorized astronauts' names and the missions they flew. Later it was sports, and I memorized all the World Series winners. A bad year in junior high school led to a suicide attempt and to my being more shy and withdrawn. I began doing more and more things by myself.

Even so, I managed to have a bit of success as an adult. I never had much problem holding down jobs. I also made a bold decision at the age of 23, moving to Arizona from Illinois. I got married at 25, having met my future wife through a newspaper personal ad. I was lucky enough at one point to be a writer for a local comedy group. Later, my wife and I had a child. Sure, I needed to deal with some issues, but I always thought they were the kind that everyone had to deal with. Until recently, I had no idea that my wife and daughter saw things in a very different light.

The hardest part about Asperger's is that it is not a physical condition. It's something you have to describe to people, and even then they may not understand what you're talking about. When I meet people for the first time, it's hard to recognize exactly when—or if—I should make my condition known. It's not like I can go up to people and say, "Hello, I'm Scott Verbout, and I have Asperger's syndrome." That seems a bit blunt. Nor can I go around with a scarlet letter "A" on my shirt at all times.

Dealing with a disorder such as Asperger's is difficult under the best of circumstances. Having to deal with it while going through the trauma of losing a job was challenging indeed. Writing this book has been a way of attempting to understand what happened to me, and to work through the feelings of inadequacy, worthlessness and depression I've had since losing my job. I figured the best way to get the negative feelings behind me was to try to reach out to other people with Asperger's, and to those people who may have loved ones with Asperger's. Those who have this condition need lots of patience and understanding.

Although it remains on the fringes of public perception, Asperger's syndrome is slowly making its way into the mainstream. In the 2009 movie *Adam*, the main character has Asperger's syndrome. He may have more exaggerated symptoms than I do, but for the most part it is a realistic portrayal of the condition. Adam is attracted to a woman who moves into his building, and after a few awkward get-togethers with her, he finally comes out and tells the woman he has Asperger's. She is taken with him enough that she decides to find out more about the condition so she can relate to him better. It would be nice if people in real life would take the time to do the same.

CHAPTER TWO:
UNDERSTANDING ASPERGER'S

Even when I was younger, I always knew there was something different about me, but I could never put my finger on it. On the outside, I look perfectly normal. On the inside is where my problem lies. And that's the most difficult part to explain to people. If you look like a normal person, people expect you to act like a normal person.

Although for the most part I'm capable of getting by in the world without assistance, certain aspects of my behavior are sometimes off-putting to other people. When I'm with a large group of people involved in a conversation, I'm likely to zone out and think about other things and not participate in whatever the group is talking about. I have difficulty picking up on nonverbal cues from others. I have trouble empathizing with people, including those in my own family. And my two main interests—sports and music—border on the obsessive.

And yet, there are positive things about Asperger's, too. I have a good eye for detail, especially when it comes to spelling and grammar, and that makes me an exceptional copy editor. And I am reliable and dependable by nature. But it's the bad things that make Asperger's such a frustrating problem to live with, the things that make me "different."

Of course, no one could tell any of this just by looking at me, which is why Asperger's syndrome is so hard to understand. When you don't act "normal," people make judgments about you. If you are more comfortable by yourself instead of with a group, others call you "antisocial," "standoffish" or "aloof." What I've learned is that people with Asperger's don't necessarily *want* to be alone. They just lack the skills needed to make friends and be more sociable. Of course, it can be a vicious cycle. If you want to be around people and try to make friends, all it takes is a few social missteps to make you feel like an outcast. Then you go back to being by yourself, thinking that it's not really worth it to be around others if it's going to be that much work.

I know all about this sort of treatment, because I've experienced it throughout my entire life. I just never knew it had a name. And then, when I finally discovered the condition called Asperger's that led to such a personal revelation about my own life, it was my awkward social behavior that contributed to my being fired from my job. Life is nothing if not ironic.

One of the key things I learned about Asperger's is that many people who have this condition also suffer from depression. I've battled depression for most of my adult life and have tried just about every kind of medication, with moderate success. I wonder now if I had known about Asperger's earlier in my life, maybe I could have dealt with my depression better. Of course, therein lies another hurdle. Even though Austrian psychiatrist Hans Asperger first documented the disorder in children in the 1940s, his work was not translated into English in the United States until 1981, and Asperger's syndrome was not recognized as a disorder by the American Medical Association until 1994. I was 32 years old in 1994, way beyond my formative years when knowing about Asperger's could have helped me through some of the pain of adolescence.

Which brings up another thing people need to understand about Asperger's: It's not a disease, so there is no cure. It's a lifelong disorder. Those who have it can work around it and try to find ways to cope, but they will never think or act like "normal" people. Even though numerous resources are available today for children who have the disorder, there is not much to help adults who have had the condition their entire lives and may not have realized it. That could change, however, as the children who have Asperger's today will become adults with Asperger's tomorrow.

Before I sat down to write this book, I had to do research. I also had to do a lot of soul-searching. Realizing that Asperger's makes it difficult for me to correctly interpret and respond to social cues, I asked family members and friends to share their impressions of me, hoping to gain a better understanding of how my condition comes across to others.

I knew that some of these descriptions might not be too flattering. One friend said she thought that writing this book was being vindictive, that I was just trying to get back at the company that fired me. There may be some truth to that, as it fits in with the Aspergian mindset. According to the book *Solutions for Adults With Asperger Syndrome* by Juanita P. Lovett, Ph.D., "many individuals with AS [Asperger's syndrome] have sympathy for people that they see as underdogs or the victims of injustice. This is probably because many people with AS have themselves had experience being mistreated by others. Growing up, they may have been bullied because of their problems with social interaction. . . . If we add to that the fact that people with AS tend to have very long memories for experiences when they have felt mistreated and usually find it hard to forgive and forget, it is easy to see why they would sympathize greatly with those whom they believe are not treated fairly."

I would say that sums up my situation quite nicely.

Yet most of the people I asked to share comments were supportive, telling me that I had something to say to people with autism who may have gone through similar experiences. One friend had this to say:

"I met Scott Verbout in 2001 when I began work at [the company]. Although I was only 21 years old, I had already been writing professionally for around three years: long enough, in other words, to know the value of a talented copy editor.

"Scott was certainly a talented copy editor. Beyond my professional gratitude for Scott's talents, however, I appreciated his subtle humor and his recognition of mine. Scott's wit and intelligence were frequently masked by his shyness, but I could appreciate that, too: I had been painfully shy until I dropped out of college and found it necessary to support myself as a reporter. (Even then, cold-calling interview subjects often left me paralyzed with dread.)

"When Scott told me he had Asperger's, I wasn't really surprised. Not long before, I had paid a visit to the medical office where my mother was then employed, and sat in on a continuing education program for physicians about autism. In it, conditions like autism and Asperger's were described as aspects of a continuum—and I left wondering how many people could really be described as 'normal.' I certainly didn't feel that I fit the description.

"That said, I felt grateful that I was far enough to the 'normal' side of the continuum that I had found it relatively simple, as an adult, to 'fit in.' Although I had often felt that I was 'playing a role' in my interactions with strangers and casual friends, it had been an easy one for me to adopt. With a biologically impaired ability to interpret social cues, Scott, I knew, had had a much tougher time.

"Over the past 10 years, Scott has been a kind and reliable friend. His attempts to meet the challenges of Asperger's head-on—in defiance of the very nature of the condition—and to use his experiences to comfort and inspire others, have only increased my respect for him. He does not have an easy life . . . but it is certainly a worthwhile one."

And this one, from another good friend:

"Scott Verbout was a copy editor when I started as a movie critic in the early 1990s—he was one-third of the finest, most eagle-eyed copy-editing desk I've ever worked with. Scott was so quiet and taciturn that at first, and for quite a while, I thought he might be unknowable. But, gradually, I got to know him, and to see that the cliché was, at least in this case, true—still waters ran deep. Scott was a man with a gentle, reflective soul and the most deadpan sense of humor. I also came to see that his remarkable copy-editing skills came not just from the rigor and thoroughness of his work habits, impressive though these were, but also from his intelligence, his knowledge and subtle understanding of the world around him."

In preparing for this book, I also read *Look Me in the Eye: My Life With Asperger's* by John Elder Robison. It was interesting to read the experiences of someone else who has Asperger's, but many of his life experiences were so different from my own that I found it hard to relate to some of the things he talked about. One similarity, though: Like me, he did not learn he had Asperger's until he was in his 40s.

Robison did offer insights about trying to communicate with "normal" people. One passage related that many people with autism are quiet and withdrawn, and this was his observation: "Many descriptions of autism and Asperger's describe people like me as 'not wanting contact with others' or 'preferring to play alone.' I can't speak for other kids, but I'd like to be very clear about my own feelings: *I did not ever want to be alone*. . . . I played by myself because I was a failure at playing with others. I was alone as a result of my own limitations, and being alone was one of the bitterest disappointments of my young life. The sting of those early failures followed me long into adulthood, even after I learned about Asperger's."

Interestingly enough, *The OASIS Guide to Asperger Syndrome* had this to say regarding people with Asperger's and sexuality: "The lack of social skills can place teens and adults with AS at risk because they may not understand the intentions of others or be able to express their own intentions clearly. . . . Men with AS, who may lack subtlety in their approach to women, are sometimes perceived as overly insistent and forward."

I hate to think that I may have been perceived that way.

Finally, it was the social networking site Facebook that may have been the deciding factor in my writing this book. When I was fired from my job, I thought at the very least I had a handful of friends at the company I could keep in touch with. I was wrong. Other than one person who had been a friend since I started working there, no one else bothered to write or call. I sent out a few e-mails. Eventually, the company blocked my incoming e-mails. It was a lonely experience. It seemed that no one even wanted to admit having known me.

Then, in the fall of 2008, I signed up on Facebook. After a while, I started searching for people I had worked with in the past, but who had left the company before I did. It turned out many people not only remembered me, but actually *liked* me! I was truly happy that I got so many wonderful replies (I've included some in the Epilogue of the book). I was worried that I was all alone in the world, that no one cared if I lived or died.

In some ways, I didn't care, either. In fact, plenty of times I thought it would be better if I were dead. Then I would be out of the way, and everyone else could go on with their lives. Yes, I really believed that. Sometimes, I still do. That's the trouble with Asperger's combined with depression. There are times when all seems lost and hopeless. I spent about 10 years going through a terrible depression. It wasn't until I discovered my Asperger's that I thought my life actually may have a purpose. I've gone through a lot of pain, and maybe if I could shed light on this condition, other people could benefit from my experiences.

When I started writing this book, I asked my parents for some of their thoughts about what I was like as a child, and if any signs suggested that I was different from other kids. Here was one of my mom's recollections:

"Scott's drawing ability was uncanny. If he saw it, he could draw it. At the age of 3, he asked me to draw his favorite heroes onto paper, and we went through quite a bit of shelf lining paper to give every superhero his allotted space. I must have drawn a hundred copies, but Scott was watching every stroke I made. Soon he was drawing Batman, Robin, Superman and Roger Ramjet by himself and coloring them in. When he turned 4, I couldn't tell the difference between my drawings and his."

One aspect of Asperger's syndrome is having intense interests. I had a few of those interests as a child, but mainly I was into the space program, big time. I was not quite 7 years old when Apollo 11 landed on the moon in July of 1969. That was probably the defining event of my childhood. After watching that, I was hooked. I studied and read all I could about the space program, as my mom remembers.

"Scott became extremely interested in the NASA space program in the late 1960s. He read *We Reach the Moon*, an adult book of 300 pages, during second grade and often wrote insightful letters to NASA. By the time the Mercury, Gemini and Apollo programs came to an end, Scott knew every flight number, every astronaut's name, and exactly which flight he rode on.

"To say that Scott was a walking encyclopedia in regard to the space program, dinosaurs, baseball, and music is an understatement. His knowledge of all these subjects was flawless, and to top it off, he could spell even the longest dinosaur's name perfectly. He knew all the states by the age of 2 and could put them correctly into a United States puzzle."

Among my mom's other memories was this story about a challenging time that I had in my very first year of life.

"When Scott was nine months old, he got *very* sick. He contracted whooping cough from the kid who lived on the lower level of our apartment building even though Scott never met him! Scott got the virus through our vents somehow. His dad and I couldn't figure out what was wrong with him and we took him to see several doctors. All the young doctors treated Scott for tonsillitis, but his cough kept getting worse. He was fighting for his very breath.

"Finally, Grandma mentioned that we should take Scott to see a doctor in Peoria, Illinois [where we lived at the time]. He listened to Scott breathe, took his vitals and ordered a blood test right away. He knew that day that Scott had whooping cough and got him onto the right medicine and told me to stop feeding him real milk. Milk was making Scott worse! The doctor told us that whooping cough was a disease that had been eradicated through DPT shots for babies (which we knew nothing about) and Scott was the first case to come along in years! Only a doctor who had seen it all would have known enough to order a blood test to determine if Scott had pertussis. He saved Scott! Most infants die from the effects of this disease.

"Despite Scott's struggles, and during his recovery, he decided to start walking! Scott was 10 months old, and we were so proud of him!"

Did pertussis have anything to do with my autistic disorder? I have no idea. But I must have been very strong to have survived that illness. After my mom told me this story, I mentioned to her that maybe I lived because I was meant to have a purpose in life. And maybe that purpose was to make people more aware of Asperger's syndrome.

CHAPTER THREE:
GROWING UP

"Is something wrong?" she said.
"Of course there is."
"You're still alive," she said.
"Oh, but do I deserve to be? Is that the question?"

—Pearl Jam, "Alive"

Although I know that Asperger's syndrome is a lifelong condition, I seemed to have a rather normal childhood. I had my share of problems, as all kids do, but for the most part, I remember being a happy child. I had friends, did well in school, and had a pleasant family life. I never felt like I didn't "fit in."

In junior high, I started noticing that I was a bit different. Junior high begins a very social time in most children's lives, and I've never been a social person. I had friends, sure, but I mostly kept to myself. In eighth grade, I had a wonderful teacher for an American History class. This guy could have been a standup comedian. He was always cracking me up, and made the class fun and enjoyable. That was probably the best class I ever had in school.

In the summer after my eighth-grade year, the city in which I lived redrew the school boundaries, forcing me to go to a different school for ninth grade. In my town, ninth grade was still considered part of junior high, and the high school comprised 10th, 11th and 12th grades. So the year after I had what may have been my favorite class ever, I had to deal with the uncertainty of going to a different school.

It was not easy. The school I had gone to for seventh and eighth grades was a brand-new school. In fact, my seventh-grade year was the first year for the school. The school to which I was being sent was a lot older, and depressing. Even though some of my friends had been caught up in the redistricting and were also sent to this school, it seemed like I had the toughest time making the transition.

It wasn't long before I began to have real problems. Maybe I was trying too hard to fit in, and maybe I said some things to some people I shouldn't have, but I began to get beat up and singled out by all the tough guys at school. Every day, it seemed, was a new introduction to hell. If you've ever seen the movie *My Bodyguard*, that was my life in ninth grade. I could not concentrate on my schoolwork. I was just trying to survive. Most of the bullying took place in P.E. class, as very little monitoring by teachers took place. It seemed a new threat always arose from someone in the class about what would happen to me the next day. I remember a day when I was so scared to go to my P.E. class that I almost passed out.

That was the year I experienced my first problems with depression. It was a miserable year, and I had no answers for how to make things better. It was around that time that I started thinking about killing myself. I came home from school after a particularly bad day, and I really had intentions of doing myself harm. I was all alone in the house, and I sat on my bed. I held a knife at my stomach and was ready to plunge it in.

I couldn't go through with it, of course. I was much too scared. I started crying and put the knife away. But my mother still remembers a comment I made sometime later, that all the knives in the house were too dull. That must have been the moment that she decided that my problems were serious indeed.

She took me to a psychiatrist soon after that, and the doctor started me on antidepressants. I was 14 years old at the time. I was still going to school, but things weren't getting much better. Finally, a decision was made that I would be kept out of school for the last two months of the school year and repeat ninth grade at my former school, where I had enjoyed seventh and eighth grades. This meant I had to get a boundary exemption to go to my former school, and my parents had to supply transportation. The next year, my mom dropped me off at school every morning and picked me up every afternoon. It wasn't a perfect year, but it was much better than the one before. I made new friends, and I was reunited with my favorite teacher. And somehow I lived with the stigma of having to repeat a grade, not because I wasn't smart enough, but rather for my own safety. Because I was so smart as a child, my mother had started me in kindergarten when I was 4 years old instead of 5. So because I had to repeat ninth grade, I ended up graduating in the class I should have been in anyway.

So what saved me? Why didn't I go through with killing myself that day in my bedroom? Aside from the potential sight of blood unnerving me, I started thinking about all the things I'd miss. I tried to come up with something that I could turn into a positive. It may sound silly to some people, but I started thinking about baseball. I'd always been a baseball fan, but lately it had become another of my obsessions. I thought if I were to kill myself, I would never know who won the World Series that year. Or ever again.

I still doubt that I would have had the nerve to go through with it. Back then, though, I was at a point where I didn't know what to do, and I figured at the time that ending my life would be easier than dealing with my problems.

I never cared about my schoolwork again, getting mostly C's and D's through high school. I thought of dropping out many times. I never considered going to college.

I believe myself to be a person of above-average intelligence, but I'll never believe that the bad things that happened to me during that terrible year served any useful purpose. That's probably when I first started distancing myself from people. I had been hurt so deeply by so many people that I was afraid to get close to anyone. The physical scars of those days are long gone, but the emotional scars remain.

I've continued to battle depression, though if I had known about Asperger's back then, it may have made things somewhat easier. Even though I continue to take antidepressant medication, the thought of suicide still crosses my mind from time to time. But it usually goes away just as quickly. I sometimes wonder, à la Jimmy Stewart in *It's a Wonderful Life*, what things might be like if I were gone. It pleases me to note that I've never come as close to killing myself as I did that long-ago day in my bedroom.

By the way, the year I tried to kill myself was 1977. The New York Yankees won the World Series that year.

CHAPTER FOUR:
LIVING WITH ASPERGER'S

Shortly after I discovered I had Asperger's, I told a friend of mine about it. He had always thought I was rather smart, and he knew a bit about Asperger's from watching a character on the TV show *Boston Legal*. I had not seen the show, but my friend explained the character to me, how he was of above-average intelligence but had odd tics. My friend said that if he had to have a disorder, Asperger's wouldn't be so bad. I thought his comment funny, but I tried to convey to him that even though I wouldn't trade my intelligence for anything, having Asperger's can be a lonely existence. It's painfully hard for me to make friends, or to know how to act in certain situations. Would I trade brains for a few more friends? Why can't I have both? That's the dilemma I face a lot of the time.

Of course, just knowing about Asperger's doesn't always help. Sometimes, it's still difficult for me to read other people and communicate with them.

Case in point: After I was fired from my previous job, I took a position with a community newspaper in town. The woman whose place I was taking had been promoted, and she trained me how to do her job. She was gracious and helpful, and we got along well. I thought we were friends.

A few months after I started at the paper, she and her husband moved out of state. Even so, she kept in touch for a few months. Then I didn't hear anything from her for almost a year.

I'd heard rumors that she had moved back to town, but I hadn't had any communication with her directly. I decided to do an Internet search for her name and see what came up. It turned out that she was teaching at a private school in town. I called one day and left a message, but after a week went by and I hadn't heard from her, I wasn't sure she had gotten the message. Because the school wasn't too far out of my way, I decided to stop by in person to leave a message for her with a secretary. I also left my cell phone number. A few days later, she called. I missed the call, but she left a message on my voice mail. She told me that my coming to her work made her uncomfortable, especially because we hadn't spoken in almost a year, and she said she never wanted me to contact her again.

I was heartbroken. After everything I had gone through with being fired from my previous job, I thought I was fortunate to land the job at the community paper, and fortunate as well to meet such a nice person. To have her react like she did stunned me. It was obvious to me that I don't have the first clue about how to read other people.

Unwritten Rules of Social Relationships, by two autistic people, Dr. Temple Grandin and Sean Barron, is a guide to help people with autism in social situations. The authors list 10 "unwritten rules," among them "Being Polite Is Appropriate in Any Situation," "Know When You're Turning People Off" and "People Are Responsible for Their Own Behaviors." I found Rule No. 6 very telling: "Not Everyone Who Is Nice to Me Is My Friend." Sounds reasonable, doesn't it? It seems that I just don't get it, allowing myself to get hurt again, most recently by the "friend" described above. No matter how hard I try, I just cannot figure out people.

Another misconception about people with Asperger's is that they don't experience feelings. Quite the contrary, we feel things very deeply. It's just that we have difficulty expressing our feelings. I like to think I'm a good person, and I try hard not to hurt people. But sometimes I do hurt people, most of the time without realizing it. When I'm told that something I've said or done has hurt someone, I am remorseful about it, usually beating myself up about it for days.

Some people don't know how to deal with Asperger's at all. I'm sure if it were a physical affliction, such as cancer, people would be better able to handle it. Because it's a psychological problem, it seems to be harder to grasp. A stigma is attached to mental illness in our society, and I'm not sure why that is. Mental disorders should be treated with as much care and understanding as physical ones.

How can I explain it? I have Asperger's syndrome, which is a form of autism. It's a high-functioning type of autism, and I don't go around saying "Five minutes to Wapner," or anything like that, but it is still autism. It just means that my brain processes information in a different way, and I do not always respond or react in the acceptable norm.

I don't know if it's another Aspergian trait, but I like to avoid confrontation whenever possible. I don't like to argue, and I usually let people have their way, even when I know I'm right. It's probably another manifestation of my poor self-esteem.

One thing common to most people with Asperger's is the importance of routine. I started thinking about my own life, my day-to-day activities, and I realized that it's true. I like to follow a schedule, and when that schedule is disrupted, it can throw everything off. Even a slight change in routine can mess up my whole day.

When I had a job working during the day, I would get ready in the morning every day in precisely the same order: shower, shave, get dressed, eat breakfast, brush teeth. Later, when I got a job working afternoons and evenings, my morning schedule was completely thrown off. Because I didn't have to be at work until mid-afternoon, I usually would eat breakfast first, then lounge around watching TV. I'd take a shower whenever I felt like it, and then sometimes I'd go to work without shaving. Just like that, a simple break in routine could disrupt my entire day.

The most significant instance I can recall about a seemingly minor change really messing up my self-ordered life was a few years ago when my wife decided to paint the walls of our downstairs bathroom. The walls had always been a light color, and I came home one night to find that she'd painted the walls beige. That was fine with me. She mentioned adding another color as "texture" to one of the walls, but I didn't think much about it until I came home the next night. She had tried to add a little maroon by using a sponge-painting technique. It didn't work out the way she had planned. So I arrived home the next night from work to find that she had painted the entire wall a dark maroon. An "accent" color, she called it. I was aghast. I don't know what I expected, but I certainly did not expect this.

After the wall was painted, I dreaded going into that bathroom. It was dark and depressing, and I hated it. Finally, after I had complained about the color for a few days, my wife relented and painted over the maroon to make that wall the same beige color as the other walls. I was happy once again.

This incident took place before I knew I had Asperger's, but as I look back on it now, it can all be traced back to a simple change in routine. I can still recall walking into that bathroom when the wall was painted maroon. It was so dark that turning on the light was necessary, even during the day, and a wave of depression would come over me as soon as I entered. I can't remember experiencing anything like that before or since.

Now that I know about Asperger's, I've had these "moments" less often, but every once in a while, they happen. I try to deal with them as best I can. Knowing about Asperger's has been the easy part of the battle. Dealing with it has been a bit harder.

CHAPTER FIVE: DEPRESSION

Back in Chapter Three, I mentioned how I first had problems with depression during my horrible ninth-grade year. After I finished high school, those feelings went away for a while. I had a series of good jobs, met a few really good people, and seemed to get along fairly well. I would have the occasional down period, as all people do, but I never again reached the point of trying to kill myself.

In 1986, I moved to Arizona, met the woman who became my wife, and everything seemed to be great. In 1991, I started a job where I would remain for more than 15 years. I was a copy editor, which was something I had never done before, but I had a terrific supervisor who taught me everything I needed to know. I had a good grasp of English, but my supervisor taught me some of the finer points. At times I was worried that I wouldn't do a good enough job because I never went to college; and it was, indeed, a difficult job to learn. But my boss was encouraging, assuring me that most people learn the basics of language and grammar in grade school. If I hadn't learned it by then, no amount of college education was going to help me. That made me feel a lot better, like she was on my side. She helped me a great deal, both professionally and personally.

It was in 1990 and 1991 that things got to be rather tense between my wife and me. My wife wanted a child, and I did not. We went back and forth on that issue for quite some time. I had reasons for not wanting children, but I knew it meant a lot to my wife, and so, eventually, I agreed. We planned our child carefully, and my wife got pregnant in late 1991. Our daughter, whom we named December, was born in August of 1992.

Most of 1992 was quite memorable. The whole process of going through my wife's pregnancy was actually kind of fun. I did all the husbandly things, and I really got into it. I went with my wife to the doctor to listen to the baby's heartbeat, I went with her when she had the ultrasound, and we went through the birthing classes, too. And my daughter's birth was certainly an experience I'll never forget.

The first few weeks after December was born were quite interesting. We had visits from several family members to help out with things. We were extremely popular for a month or so. My wife, Teresa, was on maternity leave for two months, so she was able to take care of things pretty well. It was after she went back to work that reality started setting in. I suddenly had to help out with the baby, and I didn't know how. It never came naturally for me, and I became more and more frustrated.

Certainly, more factors were involved in my being unhappy than just having a child. But in the summer and fall of 1992, that was the single biggest event going on in our lives. As the new year approached, I became increasingly aware that I was getting older, I had a baby to take care of, and there were still things I wanted to do with my life. And more and more, it looked like I would never be able to do some of those things. It's tough to look in the mirror, to realize that you're 30 years old, and you haven't really done anything with your life. It was about January of 1993 that my depression deepened again. As I've mentioned, I had gone through periods of depression before and had always managed to fight through it on my own. So when I started feeling depressed this time, I thought the same thing would happen. I figured that it was just a down cycle in my life, and that it would eventually go away.

That's why I didn't seek help immediately. When I finally did see a counselor for the first time, in May of 1994, I had been feeling depressed for more than a year.

I don't know what I expected by seeing a counselor, but I guess I was hoping for a miracle cure. I only had three visits with the first counselor, because that's all the health insurance would cover. When that was over, I saw my physician and was prescribed Prozac.

I had heard a lot about Prozac, good and bad, so I didn't know what to expect with that, either. Maybe it affects people differently, but I never felt that my overall attitude changed after I started taking it.

I saw another counselor shortly after that, and I saw her about once a month for five months. I stayed on the Prozac for six months, even doubling the dosage at one point, but I gave it up after I became convinced it wasn't helping.

I stopped seeing the counselor at the end of 1994 because, once again, the insurance coverage ran out. After almost a year of seeking outside help, I don't know if it did any good at all. I started to feel better on a few occasions, but I don't know if it had anything to do with the medication or just that I was in a good mood on a particular day.

It also was around that time that I became keenly aware of how much I was distancing myself from people. I had very few friends at work, or anywhere else, for that matter. That's where a lot of the frustration originated—not having anyone I thought I could talk to. I was in need of a good friend.

Friends can come in any shape or form. Sometimes, all a person needs is for someone to listen to him. As I mentioned above, I was fortunate to have a boss who also was a good friend and mentor. This woman was about 12 years my senior, but we shared a lot of the same interests. Of course, being copy editors, we both loved the nuances of the English language. And we were both really into the space program. In fact, when I applied for the job as a proofreader, I had to take a test. As luck would have it, the test was a movie review of a documentary about the space program. I can't say I got a great score on the test, but I did catch several factual errors about the space program that the average person might have missed. It was as if I was meant for that job.

I had my struggles early on, as it was a difficult job, but my boss seemed to believe in me, and that meant a lot. It was during this time that my depression was back full force. My boss probably knew something was wrong, but she never said anything. Then one Sunday we both had to work. We got done, and then spent some time chatting. I just poured my heart out to her, about my depression, about most everything. She was sympathetic and listened to every word. After that, she was more like a friend than a boss.

How good of a friend was she? One story sums it up for me. In the summer of 1995, my father-in-law was dying of cancer. He was in Nebraska, and my wife and I lived in Arizona. At the time, our daughter was about 3 years old. My wife flew back to Nebraska several times that summer to see her father. She decided to take advantage of the Labor Day holiday weekend to fly back one more time. She took our daughter on the trip as well. (My father-in-law passed away in November of 1995.)

It just so happened that our wedding anniversary was over Labor Day weekend. It was the first time my wife and I had been separated on an anniversary. My boss knew I was going to be all alone, so she invited me to go out to dinner with her and her husband. It was a nice gesture, and I've never forgotten that.

Although I had stopped seeing the counselor by the end of 1994, probably the best thing about my experience with seeking help was that my counselor suggested I keep a journal of my thoughts, which I did. Of course, at that time I had no idea what Asperger's syndrome was. I just thought I was going through a hellish depression.

In researching this book, I went back to that journal some 14 years after I wrote it. It began like this:

"The following is a story of unhappiness, depression and unfulfilled dreams, about a person coming completely unraveled."

Some of the entries still hold true after all these years. Some don't, which must mean I'm getting better. Although I don't claim to be a poet, I decided to write my journal in poetry style. Here's one entry, titled "Depression":

It's difficult to describe, though I'm sure most people have gone through it.
It's like walking around with a cloud over your head.
It's waking up and not being able to get out of bed because you feel the weight of the world on your shoulders.
It's constantly worrying about what you're going to do with your life,
Or worrying that you might make the wrong choice.
It's not being able to talk to others about it, for fear that you'll bring them down, too.
It's the feeling of total hopelessness.
It's feeling that nobody loves you.
It's feeling so overwhelmed that you can't do even the simplest of chores.
It's the feeling that you'll never be happy again.
It's the feeling that you're being a burden to everyone else.
It's the feeling that whatever you do doesn't really matter.
It's when even the things you used to enjoy don't bring happiness anymore.
It's the feeling that things can't possibly get worse, but they always do.
It's the feeling that if you were to die, nobody would really miss you.
And that killing yourself might actually be a good idea.
It's feeling like a disinterested bystander as life passes you by.

As I reread my journal, all the while I kept wondering what might have been if I had known about Asperger's all along. How would my life have been different? Could I have better handled my depression?

For instance, this passage is from the introduction to my journal:

"I have very few friends, and a lot of that is because of me. I have never been able to get close to people on a personal level. I am uncomfortable in social situations, and I'm quite happy being by myself. In the last year, I have seen counselors and taken medication."

If my counselors had known about Asperger's back then, I'm sure those sentences would have raised a red flag immediately about my condition. Alas, no one ever mentioned it to me.

And then harsh reality sets in: Since I found out about Asperger's, my life hasn't changed substantially. I still get depressed, and I still have problems communicating and dealing with others. The only difference is that now I know *why* these things are happening. But as far as being able to cope with these problems, I'm not much better off than I was before.

CHAPTER SIX:
MUSIC

I want it all to go away, I want to be alone
Sympathy's wasted on my hollow shell.
I feel there's nothing left to fight for
No reason for a cause
And I can't hear your voice, and I can't feel you near.

— Sarah McLachlan, "Lost"

In earlier chapters, I mentioned how music has been an almost obsessive interest with me. Although I didn't know about Asperger's syndrome until recently, my obsession with certain songs and singers ties in with the feelings of depression I've had for most of my life. The thing that people need to know about depression is that it is a disease, as much as cancer is a disease. But for some reason, it's harder for people to grasp depression as an ailment. Tell someone you have cancer, and people will send you sympathy cards and flowers. Tell someone you suffer from depression, and you're more likely to get a blank stare. Would it be better to be in a wheelchair? At least then people could see that something was wrong. Depression, like Asperger's syndrome, is a different kind of beast.

You may be wondering what this has to do with music. The simple answer is, when I was at my lowest point, when I felt like I had nowhere else to turn, music was the one thing that got me through those tough times. Without music, there's a chance I wouldn't be here today. There is no miracle cure for depression, and while I don't claim that music has been a cure, in my case, it most definitely has been a comfort.

It's difficult to convey to others the sheer hopelessness one feels when suffering from depression. I liken it to walking through life in a fog. So it follows that the kind of music that has had the biggest influence on me is the kind that reflects the things I'm feeling. And there is one singer in particular who has had a significant impact on me.

Because of a series of personal problems, I was at a low point in 1994. I remember vividly that I was watching VH1 one afternoon, half asleep, only to be roused by a video featuring a beautiful woman in a dark-colored dress. It was a simple performance video, but it had me mesmerized. When the video was finished, I caught the name of the song—"Possession"—and the singer—Sarah McLachlan. The name didn't mean much to me, as I'd never heard of her before. A few weeks later, I was in my car, driving to a doctor's appointment where I would be given my first prescription for Prozac, when "Possession" came on the radio. I recognized it immediately as the song from the video. And then, about an hour or so later, as I waited at the drugstore for my prescription to be filled, "Possession" came over the pharmacy's sound system. Surely, hearing the song three times so close together had to be a sign of better days to come.

I've often thought that depressed people have their own unique language. When I was at my lowest point, I thought that I was the only person in the world who was feeling so miserable. I didn't think anyone else could possibly understand. As I got deeper and deeper into Sarah McLachlan's music, I began to pick out lyrics that seemed to sum up exactly what I was feeling but could not put into words.

Some of the lyrics to Sarah's songs hit so close to home, it was eerie. This passage from the song "Out of the Shadows" comes about the closest to describing the way I felt at the time: "The hours pass so slowly/The life's slipping out of me/No way's the right way/Is there a way out for me?/My life's slipping out."

From that moment on, Sarah's music became essential to my well-being. Little did I know the day that I first saw her video on TV how prophetic these lyrics from "Possession" would be: "My body aches to breathe your breath/Your words keep me alive."

Although Sarah McLachlan has been the most influential singer to me, there have been others—Natalie Merchant, Melissa Etheridge, Fiona Apple and Patty Griffin have all written songs that, at one time or another, had a profound effect on me. I do have some favorite male singers—Bruce Springsteen, John Mellencamp, Billy Joel—but when it comes to putting all their emotions into a song, in my opinion, female singer-songwriters simply do it better.

In the spring and summer of 1998, I was going through another especially rough time. That year, Natalie Merchant's *Ophelia* album was released. One song in particular stood out for me—"The Living," which was told from the perspective of someone contemplating suicide. The song gave me chills the first time I heard it, and it has the same effect on me to this day. I don't know whether Natalie herself has ever been in that position, but because I have, her words struck me as coming from someone who really understood those feelings: "I'll go off, I'll make myself scarce/ Come tomorrow you won't find me here/'Cause I don't care to stay with the living."

Not the most uplifting stuff, I know. But that's the kind of music that appealed to me when I was at my lowest point. People sometimes ask me if listening to this kind of music might make me even *more* depressed. While I can't deny that that argument has merit, I suppose at the time, I figured it was better to feel sad than to feel nothing at all.

Depression for me has been an ongoing battle, one that I'll probably have to deal with for the rest of my life. It's a tough road, and not a fun one to walk down, but I'm sure someone somewhere, at this very moment, is feeling a lot worse than I do. And one day, that person may write a song about it.

CHAPTER SEVEN: MARRIAGE AND FAMILY

"There's Got to Be a Reason"
Sure, there are times when raising a child has been a struggle,
But I do love my daughter.
When I was at my lowest points,
When I very easily could have ended it all,
I didn't, because I want to see my daughter grow up.
I would never want her to think it was her fault that I wasn't around anymore,
Just because some things got a little hard to deal with.
So I guess if there's one thing I'm living for right now,
It would be my daughter.

— from my journal

I'm very glad that I have a strong and loving family. Even when I felt that nobody else liked me, I always knew my family did. My parents, my grandparents, my aunts and uncles have always been close. And it's comforting to know that if my wife and I were to lose everything tomorrow, we could probably return home and feel welcome.

Sometimes, I wonder what I would be like if my parents had divorced, or if I had lost one or both parents at an early age. I think I'm pretty screwed up the way it is, and I don't know if I would be totally insane by now or if those experiences might have made me stronger.

My paternal grandparents, especially, are people I admire greatly. Since 1993, they've been hosting family reunions nearly every other year. I'm sure it must be quite expensive to do this, but for them it's worthwhile. We always enjoy going back to see everyone. It's a great way to stay connected to people who I might have lost track of after I moved away from home.

But of course, the people closest to me are my wife and daughter. They've seen the best and worst of me. They've been there for me ever since I discovered I had Asperger's syndrome. And they were there for me when I suffered the trauma of losing my job.

Here's another entry from my journal about my wife.

"Teresa"
As I write this [1994], Teresa and I have been married for more than six years
And have known each other for more than eight years.
I love her very much, although it bothers me lately that we don't want the same things out of life.
I value our marriage, and Teresa is the kind of person I always wanted to find—
She's nice, she's friendly, she has a good sense of humor, and she loves me.
I know I am very lucky to have her as my wife.
If I had it to do all over again,
I'd probably still marry her.
Only next time, I would get the issue of children resolved first.
One night Teresa got out a letter that I had written when we were first dating.
Of course, it was mushy and sweet,
But it made me think back to those days.
What I wrote in that letter was the way I really felt then.
It felt so good to be in love,
To learn about and enjoy the company of another person.
Unfortunately, that feeling doesn't last forever.
I still love my wife, but being in love is not the same as falling in love.
There's a newness about discovering that special person
That years of marriage and children can't bring back.
And that's too bad.
Because when I think back on the time Teresa and I first met,
I can honestly say that I was happy.
Really happy.
And there haven't been many times in my life before or since that I can say that about.

I got married at the age of 25. For the most part, I enjoy married life. I haven't once regretted my decision to marry Teresa. But for any married couple, disagreements happen, even when one partner doesn't have Asperger's syndrome. It wasn't until my wife and I had been married for 18 years that I discovered I had Asperger's. Imagine the disagreements and misunderstandings over the years, perhaps more than the average.

I must say, before going on, that I love my wife and daughter very much. There is nothing I wouldn't do for either of them. But there were times, especially when I was deeply depressed, that things became almost too much for me to handle.

As I mentioned in Chapter Five, my wife and I had disagreements about whether to have a child at all. I finally agreed to have one, and my daughter arrived in August of 1992.

Things bothered me about the way Teresa acted toward me after our daughter was born, though. I didn't often tell Teresa how I felt then, but I had let her know repeatedly beforehand that I wasn't thrilled about having kids. And when the baby was born, I struggled as I always figured I would. I assumed that my wife was better prepared for everything than I was because she had always wanted kids. Now I understand that some of my struggles with fatherhood were directly related to my condition and the importance of routine in my life.

To me, it seemed that Teresa expected me to do things automatically, without having to be told. Well, I hadn't been around babies that much before we had ours, so I really didn't know how to take care of one. I always tried my best, but I got the impression that Teresa expected me to do more. When I would let her know how I was feeling, about how the baby had completely altered my life, Teresa would always say it wasn't that bad. She would say that, all things considered, we had a well-behaved baby. She would always try to tell me how I should feel. And of course, a neurotypical husband and father probably would have understood and sympathized—after all, she had to go through the same things. Instead, I got the impression that she didn't care what I was going through.

Other things bothered me, too—things that are minor to a lot of people, but disproportionately important to someone with Asperger's. There were things that had always made me happy, things that I enjoyed doing, that I couldn't do anymore. For example, I had always been a big sports fan, and I would always watch games on weekends, I would always watch the World Series and Super Bowl, and Teresa would always complain. I never really expected her to enjoy sports as much as I did, but I hoped she would at least take a passing interest because it meant so much to me. She never did, and I took this personally.

I had trouble adjusting to the demands of a newborn in other ways, too. I couldn't understand why Teresa expected me to drop everything I was doing when she needed help with the baby, although I was usually willing to help if I could. But then I was offended that when it came to something I was interested in, she couldn't be bothered with it.

At that time, my job involved working lots of Saturdays and Sundays. Eventually, I started looking forward to working weekends, mostly so I could have some time to get my frazzled brain together. So I didn't get to enjoy a lot of the things I used to, but I figured it was for the best. I've noted earlier that Asperger's sufferers frequently have an obsessive interest in topics such as sports. There was a time when I had an in-depth knowledge about sports, but with a crying baby in the house, I couldn't enjoy watching the games at home, so I stopped following them as much as I once did.

In the year after our daughter arrived, my wife started talking about having another child. By this time, I was well into my depression, and I didn't want to hear about having another child.

Another journal entry:

"Fatherhood"
I never pictured myself as being a father
And sometimes I still don't.
I have a beautiful daughter, and I know she will grow up to be a beautiful woman.
But it's been a difficult road for me.
Not that I thought it would be easy, but I guess I wasn't prepared for it emotionally.
I'm not an outwardly emotional person, and being a father has been draining.
I've never been responsible for the life of another human being before.
It can be a little scary.
It's only been a little more than two years, and I feel like I have nothing left to give.
I ask myself, if it's like this now, after two years,
What's it going to be like in 10 years? Or 15?
And this is only one child we're talking about.
My wife still wants another.
I really don't think I would be able to handle that.
If I had to go through all of this again,
I think I would go completely insane.

To put it mildly, parenthood has not gone exactly as I had planned. Asperger's sufferers are easily frazzled by disruptions to their daily routines, and few disruptions can be greater than having a child. I don't know for sure how I expected it would be, but it has been a difficult challenge for me. I don't want to make it sound like I don't love my daughter, because I do. But just like every other aspect of Asperger's syndrome, raising a child has been like an otherworldly experience.

In preparing to write this book, I asked both my wife and my daughter to share their perspectives of what it's like to live with someone who has Asperger's syndrome. At first my daughter was hesitant because she thought I would get upset by what she wrote. But I encouraged her to do it anyway, because I realized that I probably wasn't aware of some of the things that have bothered her in the past.

At this point, my daughter is a teenager, and it's like I don't even know who she is. Part of that has come from working a night shift for three years and not knowing what is going on in her life. Part of it also is that I don't know how to relate to her, even when we are together. She barely speaks to me, about anything.

My relationship with my daughter has been complicated by the expectations I had for her as she was growing up—expectations that were influenced by my Asperger's syndrome. Because I'm an obsessive sports fan, I thought it would be inevitable that she would grow up to be one, too. She did not. So now all of the knowledge that I have burned into my memory banks about baseball, football and all the other sports I enjoy watching has been of no use in this father-daughter relationship. I was hoping to teach her how to keep score of a baseball game, how to throw a curve ball, how to calculate batting averages, and I naturally assumed that she would share my interest in the sport that I love and grew up with—the sport that one day in my bedroom as a teenager had saved my life.

None of it seems to mean anything to my daughter, and that saddens me. Now I don't know what kind of knowledge I can impart to her that will even make a difference in her life. I have enough trivia in my head to be a contestant on *Jeopardy!*, but right now I'm not sure what I could tell my daughter that would be of interest to her. It feels like all the knowledge I have is just going to waste if I can't share it with her.

Here is another entry from my journal, written when my daughter was 2 years old:

"My Daughter"
I've done a lot of complaining about my difficulty adjusting to fatherhood,
But the truth is, my child is everything I could have hoped for.
She's tall and skinny, with long legs and long fingers:
Perfect for either a model or a basketball player.
She has blond hair and blue eyes,
Something I never thought would happen.
And December has such a cute face.
Physically, she's all I could have asked for,
So I don't want to make it sound like everything has gone wrong.
I guess I'm growing as a person as my daughter is growing.
I've done things in the last two years that I never thought I would do.
I've changed diapers,
I've taken my daughter to the doctor with ear infections,
I've stayed home with her when she had pink eye and chickenpox,
I've given her bottles and spoon-fed her.
It's all been a strange and horrifying experience,
And I'm usually not good at handling new things.
But I do love my daughter,
And I just look forward to the future,
When she'll be able to carry on a conversation,
When I'll be able to teach her things,
And when she becomes more independent.
Right now it's a struggle, but I know it will eventually get better.
I just have to keep reminding myself of that.
I guess the bottom line is this:
Am I glad I'm a father?
Yes.
Would I want to relive these last two years?
No.

One thing that has caught me off guard about raising a teenager nowadays is their dependence on technology. I don't remember being so tied down to different kinds of technology growing up, but it's impossible to find my daughter at any time without either her iPod or her cell phone. If she's not wearing her iPod headphones and blocking out the rest of the world, even when I'm trying to talk to her from the next room, then she's texting someone on her cell phone. I use text messaging on my cell phone once in a while, and usually for emergencies, but for today's teens, texting seems to have replaced speaking to someone altogether. My daughter rarely uses her phone to call someone—only to text. Even though I'm far from being the one who should be talking about interpersonal relationships, I've always felt a need to speak to someone face to face to have an impact. I know that Aspergians are famous for missing nonverbal cues, but there is something about seeing a person's facial reactions that's important to me. I actually enjoy talking to someone in person. E-mailing and texting are just too impersonal for me. It appears we are raising a generation of people who will never be able to have a face-to-face conversation with anyone. If they couldn't e-mail or text someone, today's teens would be completely lost.

I have obviously made mistakes as a parent, before and after finding out about Asperger's. Still, I have always tried to give my daughter the best possible upbringing. I think about the world my daughter is growing up in, and realize that children growing up with both parents will be in the minority. Will it be enough to give my daughter a strong, loving foundation when most other children won't have that? How will that affect her mental state?

Maybe she'll be stronger than I was and I won't have to worry about it.

"Fears"
I have a great many fears,
Though I'm not sure if I have more than anyone else.
Some of them are well-founded,
Some may not be.
But one of my reasons for not wanting kids in the beginning was that
I didn't want them to have to go through all the pain that I've been through.
I know that sounds pessimistic.
I just don't think I could bear to see someone I helped bring into this world have all the difficulties I had.
I've already been through it once.
I don't want to go through it again.

— from my journal

My wife and daughter both agreed to contribute their thoughts about what it's like to live with someone who has Asperger's syndrome. Theirs are the next two chapters that follow.

CHAPTER EIGHT:
TERESA'S CHAPTER

This chapter contains recollections from my wife, Teresa, about what it's like to live with someone who has Asperger's syndrome.

I can't count the number of times over the years I have asked myself, "What in the world did you get yourself into?" Or the times I felt stuck between a rock and a hard place.

There were many situations that I didn't imagine in my marriage. Times when my parents tried to talk to Scott and only received yes and no answers. Times I stayed up with our daughter when she was sick, and he didn't even come out to check on us. And if he did come out, he would ask "What's wrong with her?" in an irritated voice. Times when we had a communication problem, and he wouldn't open up so we could resolve it. This has not been an easy marriage. And in all honesty, not what I had expected.

Between our fifth and 15th years of marriage, I would feel bittersweet on New Year's Eve and on our anniversary. On New Year's Eve, I would wonder if this would be the year that we would break up. On our anniversary, I wondered if it was the last one. There were times I had serious doubts. And one year I had actually thought about leaving. I had even made up a budget to see if I could raise our daughter on my salary alone.

The year was 1998. Later, I would find out that it was one of Scott's lowest years with depression. For me, it was one of the lowest years in our marriage. Because he shares some journal entries in this book, I would like to share bits from a letter I wrote at that time. One night I couldn't sleep, I was so upset. I had to write down my feelings to let them out. I kept the letter in a drawer. I showed it to Scott 11 years later as I was writing this chapter.

"I feel we are unable to have the sort of marriage that I had hoped. There really isn't much between us. I do not feel loved, cherished or cared about. I feel I am nothing more than a stone around your neck; that your daughter and I are mere bugs that you have to live with.

"You probably don't even know that I feel this way. I've hinted. You kind of just laughed it off. I'm just so scared to actually come right out and say it, 'I don't feel loved and I'm not sure I want to be married to you anymore.'"

Marriage is a lot of work. When you are married to someone with depression and Asperger's syndrome, you can double that effort.

Only the beginning

While we were dating, everything seemed fine. Scott and I connected. We would actually start to say the same things, often think of the same ideas.

At first, I thought that Scott was just shy. He seemed to be an extreme introvert. My family liked to tease, and that doesn't sit well with Scott. So it's no surprise that he and my parents didn't get off to the best start. My parents saw how serious I was about him, so they tried to make an effort. When we would go back to the Midwest to visit, they tried to make conversation. They would ask about sports, his comedy group or his music, but Scott would reply with one-word answers and never expand on the conversation. After several years of trying to engage his interest, my parents eventually stopped.

And it wasn't just my parents. Even when we visited his parents, he really didn't talk a lot or expand on many topics. When our daughter was born, both sets of grandparents lived in the Midwest. I kept them up to date with regular phone visits during the pregnancy and after. It got to the point that if Scott's parents had questions about our daughter, they would ask me. When they called, often they talked to me longer than they talked to him. I think this started to bother him.

Three years after my father died, my mom and my sister and her family moved near us from Nebraska. Scott had taken vacation time from work to help with the move. I was so touched that he took his time off to help my family. Their relocation created the first time Scott and I had family who lived near us since we had been together. It was the first time I had lived near family since I had been an adult out on my own. Finally, I could have family dinners and holidays. I could just go shopping or to a movie with my mom or my sister. I could watch my nieces grow, and my daughter could grow up with her cousins.

The move was also an adjustment. I liked seeing and visiting with my family. My sister did day care in her home, and she provided after-school care to our daughter. But Scott didn't require as much visiting time with them. Sometimes, my daughter and I would go. Sometimes, Scott would come with us. I'm sure he was lonely when we went without him. As I look back on that time, I think I craved time with them because for so long it felt like I had been by myself. With his job at the time, Scott would be at work on most evenings and most weekends. And when he was home, he didn't really get into any deep conversation. He mostly watched TV.

Emotional aspects

Until the last few years, I didn't depend on Scott for emotional support. I don't know why. I just never leaned on him. I think when I was younger it was because I didn't want to emotionally lean on one man. To need someone that way. Instead, I relied on an emotional network made up of my family, a college friend and friends from work. When Scott became more depressed, he just wouldn't be able to be there for me anyway.

Through the years, my friends would change, but I still relied on them. I left my longtime job in June 2008. My sister and I hadn't been seeing each other as much as we used to. I didn't have the network like before. I started to rely on Scott more and more. I think that has made us closer, but still it's sometimes difficult to discuss issues.

Conflict resolution has always been a problem for us. If I'm upset about something and I explain what I'm upset about, Scott will usually say, "Okay." He will acknowledge my feelings but will not contribute to the resolution. Many times if I ask about his feelings on the subject, I often hear, "I don't know." I would take that as apathy. And then I would get angry.

We went through counseling a few years ago. Sometimes, I feel like I need a referee to get a resolution. What was nice about counseling was that our counselor would make Scott sort through his feelings so we could come up with a solution. Learning about Asperger's has made me realize that Scott sometimes just can't put his feelings into words. That is hard for me to understand because I can be very introspective. So now I've learned to play 20 questions. If I can get just a little more information about how he feels or thinks, maybe I can come up with a solution that will work for both of us.

Previously in the book, Scott talked about the infamous bathroom wall. We actually spent a counseling session discussing this. Through all of our marriage, Scott hasn't liked painted walls. We've had white walls, or a light off-white. When we arrange the furniture, it stays that way for years. Scott doesn't like change. When I painted the one bathroom wall maroon, Scott said he didn't like it. He said it was an ugly color. I didn't understand why he thought it was ugly because he wears an Arizona Cardinals T-shirt that is the same color. But through counseling, he was able to explain how he felt about the bathroom wall. I learned it wasn't so much the color as the intensity of the color. That maroon color is used in our patio drapes and the valances in the family room. That seems to be okay because it isn't as overpowering. I was able to paint the kitchen a very light yellow. Because it is a pale shade, it isn't overpowering to him.

Sometimes, when he is upset, Scott employs the silent treatment. I don't know if this can be attributed to Asperger's or if it's just one of Scott's personality traits. The silent treatment happens when maybe he had preconceived plans or ideas that didn't pan out. A few years ago, his parents came out during the holidays. They were staying at a hotel a few miles from our house. His mom wanted to go shopping one day, so I took her and my daughter shopping in the morning. I thought it would be an opportunity for Scott to spend time with his dad. My mother-in-law wanted to look for a bathing suit. Well, few stores carry bathing suits in December, even in Phoenix, so we were looking for quite a while. We were gone much longer than expected. I believe we called the house to give Scott updates. But when we got home late in the afternoon, he wouldn't talk to us and acted very mopey. I think he was disappointed that we were gone so long because he wanted to watch music videos with his mom. Now, he never mentioned that he wanted to watch videos at that particular time, so I wasn't aware that we needed to be home earlier. But I knew finding a bathing suit was important to my mother-in-law because she wanted to take advantage of the hot tub at the hotel.

The incident was similar to the day of our wedding. My future in-laws, my parents, my bridesmaids and I went into town to decorate the reception hall of the church. Scott stayed at my parents' house thinking his friends would come. He didn't clarify this with them. It was just his expectation. Instead, his friends went to a city at least a half-hour away to shop for wedding gifts. I wasn't happy because my groom didn't help decorate when his parents and the rest of my family did. My groom wasn't happy because he sat in a house by himself.

Even in writing this chapter, I have received a silent treatment because I did other things instead of getting my writing finished.

I'm not sure of the best way to handle the situation except to ask every day if he has plans or expectations. And when he desires something, to ask for a timetable and schedule it, like I do everything else. Or when he is being unusually quiet, try to get him to vocalize the problem and his feelings.

Obsessions

One of the traits of Asperger's is an intense interest in something. When I read this in the information Scott gave me, it was like a light bulb going off. I knew from his childhood he had an interest in the space program. He would write to NASA to ask for materials. He memorized every mission and the astronauts who manned the missions. When I met him, it was sports. I joke that we planned our wedding date around a sports schedule, but it isn't really a joke. I would never have been able to have an October wedding because of baseball playoffs and the World Series. And March was out of the question because of the NCAA college basketball tournament.

I remember in the first few years of our marriage being really angry one Saturday night. We worked all weekend and I just wanted to go out for pizza for dinner. But there was a game on that Scott didn't want to miss. So we stayed home. It seemed like there was always a game on. He would even keep a score sheet on important baseball games, like the All-Star Game. Sometimes, he would compromise if I would suggest a place that had a TV so he could follow the game. Now, I ask when the games are on so we can work around them. If I want to go to a movie, I know we need to catch a show before or after. Baseball season is the most difficult because there is a game nearly every day.

From sports, Scott moved his obsession to music; one female singer after another. Melissa Etheridge, Sarah McLachlan, Natalie Merchant, and so on. I know he mentioned how important the lyrics are to him. I find it interesting that he seems to relate only to female singers, and usually attractive ones. As the Internet grew in popularity, so did Scott's obsession. He would spend time online in a Natalie Merchant chat room. It seemed odd that a grown man in his 30s would be so interested in something like that. Scott expressed his disappointment that I didn't take enough interest. But really, I would feel angry and jealous. These women, who don't even know him, would get more attention and admiration from him than I could even dream about. Many times, I have felt like I had to compete.

What do you do when your husband watches videos and writes down lyrics but doesn't talk to you?

Sometimes, I will watch a video or a game. But once I have seen a music video, I don't really want to sit through it again. When our daughter was young, it was difficult to watch a game, although I remember following the Phoenix Suns during 1992-93, the year they went to the NBA Finals. I had a full-time job and a house and family to take care of. For the last two years, I've been working on a master's degree. I often do homework on the sectional sofa and try to follow the game while Scott is watching. I like to watch games when a hometown team plays. I don't like to watch sports just to watch sports.

When it's important, I try to schedule my responsibilities around the game. I don't have time to watch games on Saturday and Sunday. But I try to get all the chores done one day so I can watch a game the next afternoon. This was important during the 2008 football season when the Arizona Cardinals made their way to the Super Bowl.

Parenthood

Scott has discussed his difficulties with fatherhood. He mentions that he felt that I expected him to know everything. I guess I figured some things were common sense. We had baby books. Some of the books said to let the father do things his own way. Many mothers nag too much. In hindsight, I should have explained things more. I should have realized that he never took care of little cousins or baby-sat. If we had known about Asperger's then, I could have put some care instructions into a logical format so he would understand.

He would hold the baby away from his body, rather than cradling her against his chest. He would go through the mechanics of changing and feeding her. Scott would have one day off in the middle of the week. When the baby was a newborn, she would stay home with Scott that day so we could save on day-care expenses. One day I came home from work and Scott said the baby had been crying a lot. He said he had changed her diaper and fed her, but she still cried. I went to kiss her on the forehead and I could feel that she had a fever. I took her temperature and it was 101. It really scared me because I felt Scott should have known that, but he didn't. Why? Scott did not show much physical affection toward the baby. If he would have only touched her forehead or kissed her like many people do with babies, he would have felt that she was hot.

His lack of physical affection was odd to me because he often would hug and kiss me. When our daughter was young, I can remember only one time when I saw Scott kiss her. Once he was putting December in her car seat and when he was done strapping her in, I saw him kiss the top of her head. Any other time, it was December who went to her father for a hug or good-night kiss.

I knew it was challenging for Scott to relate to children. He couldn't relate to them. It's like he pushed all his memories of childhood and that simple joy that kids have out of his mind. Sometimes, his lack of understanding and empathy was embarrassing.

One night we were at a 1950s-type diner with two other couples after a softball game. Remember the old dinette seats that had a space between the vinyl back and seat cushion? December was maybe 3, and she was sliding back and forth on the chair with her legs going through the space. One time she went back too far and got stuck. She couldn't move and started to panic and fuss. I tried to free her, but I couldn't do it. Scott just sat there. He didn't get up to help me. The other two husbands who were with us got up and helped while my husband—my daughter's father—just sat there. They were able to free December.

I was embarrassed. And I was even more humiliated a few days later when one of the men, who was a co-worker at the time and a friend, asked why Scott just sat there and didn't help his daughter. I later asked Scott why he didn't do anything. He said that because December got herself stuck by messing around, she could probably get herself out of the situation. And to this day, he still feels that way. Now that I understand Asperger's more, I can see his logic. However, I don't think he took into account the emotions a 3-year-old was feeling when she was scared. Or the security children learn when they know their parents will help them when needed.

It wasn't until December was 5 that I could see Scott starting to understand and to relate to her. I would tell him that he needs to be there for her so when she was older, she would turn to him. Scott worked so many evenings and weekends that December and I formed a close emotional bond. When she has a problem, she comes to me. Now that she is older, her tendency to come to me bothers Scott because he wants to be involved in her life.

Still, I know that he loves her. There have been times when we watch old videos of when she was a toddler or baby and I don't remember when they were filmed. That's because they were done when I was at work and

Scott was home with December. He even edited a series of clips together to Elton John's song "Blue Eyes."

When she was a toddler, she caught chickenpox. Her symptoms started a few days before I had a business trip to Louisiana. I couldn't cancel the trip. Scott was going to have to handle the illness alone. Our day-care provider would still take her. All the kids there had the virus. And she was contagious before we knew she had it. Scott did really well. Fortunately, December was young enough that she really didn't itch. She had a few nights where she fussed a bit, but Scott could calm her down.

Sometimes, if I had to work on a Saturday, Scott and December would go to a movie and do fun things all day. I liked it when they had that time together. If I had a conference out of town and they came with me, their schedule was sleeping in and seeing the local sights.

I've seen Scott pat December on the back when he coached her YMCA basketball team, the flower he brought home for her when she made the junior high basketball team, the pride when she wins a tennis match and the tears he shed with her when she had her first heartbreak.

Scott mentions that I talked a lot about having a second child. I remember talking about it here and there, but I don't remember pushing the subject. My sister and I were close growing up, and I wanted my daughter to have that type of relationship. But my husband reminded me one day that there was no guarantee that siblings would be close. I knew he was right. I've seen lots of examples where siblings weren't close at all.

When December was 2, I made the decision not to have another child. I felt our marriage wouldn't survive the stress. If we divorced, I didn't think I had the energy or emotional strength to raise two kids by myself and work full time. I decided it was better for my daughter to grow up with her father than to have a sibling. Yes, sometimes I wish December had a sister to turn to. But I've learned to appreciate the closeness of the three of us together.

Discovery

When Scott first handed me the list of Asperger's symptoms, I felt relief. I was relieved to learn that maybe there was a "reason" for his behavior and that I didn't marry someone who, at times, could be so insensitive. The lack of empathy was something that greatly bothered me. How could this man who was so sweet and attentive when we were dating, when it was just the two of us, be uncaring to others' feelings?

During the past five years, Scott has become more social. I think some of it is because of the combination of medicines he is on. He and my mother get along better. I wish my dad had lived long enough to know Scott this way. My father passed away in 1995, a few months after our seventh wedding anniversary. Our daughter was 3 at the time. I wish my dad could have seen Scott as the father he is now.

Now that we know more about Asperger's, Scott makes a more conscious effort. For me, I have to learn not to take certain behaviors so personally. Sometimes, it's very difficult. I try not to write him off as being uncaring. I've learned that if I need some emotional support or help, sometimes I need to clearly state my desires. Joking and hinting around don't work.

I'm extremely proud of how he wants to share his story about Asperger's syndrome. He received many compliments when he first wrote about the disorder in a newspaper article. And he spent a lot of time writing this book. A recent article in our local newspaper explained that many of the children diagnosed with autism are becoming adults and entering the work force. What about those adults who have gone through their whole life feeling different but not knowing why? What about the grown-up undiagnosed children? Scott wants to help others who may be going through the same hell that he has felt. His desire to help illustrates the same gentle and caring soul I fell in love with.

CHAPTER NINE: DECEMBER'S CHAPTER

My daughter gets her turn to share her thoughts about growing up with a father who has Asperger's syndrome.

In this chapter, I will tell my side of the issues my dad has brought up about me and I will finally be able to say all of the things that I have waited many years to say. And I will finally be able to tell my dad everything he has done that has bothered me.

First of all, to say that I am not interested in sports is a huge misconception! I started playing tee ball when I was 4 and the next year joined a soccer team. After that, I didn't really play a lot of sports except for throwing the football around with dad in the backyard and learning the different plays like the "Statue of Liberty" play. Then in fifth grade, I went to my best friend's basketball game. She played in a YMCA league, and while I was sitting on the bleachers, the coach came by and asked me if I wanted to play. Because we were really young, nobody was very competitive. I had absolutely no idea what I was doing! I had never played the game before so I mostly just stood there and watched everyone pass the ball back and forth. After that, I got into basketball and signed up for the YMCA league. I played for four years, being on several different teams with several different coaches. Dad even coached one season, which was pretty fun.

Once I got into junior high, I also tried out for basketball in seventh and eighth grade and made the "B" team (which is pretty much second string) both years. I was disappointed that I didn't make first string, but I went to a big school, so I was glad that I had just made a team. In eighth grade, I tried out for volleyball as well, but didn't make it, and I also tried out for softball and made the "B" team again. I wasn't the best player on the team. There was someone always faster than I was, someone always stronger than I was, and someone always there to make a basket or catch the ball when I wasn't. And I always knew dad noticed that. At least, that's how I saw it.

One season when I was in the YMCA league, there was a girl on my team that my dad really took to. He would praise everything she did. I would be lying if I said that I never got jealous. I started resenting her, which was hard to do because she was, to this day, one of the nicest people I have ever met in my life. She always had something friendly to say about everyone. And I hated that I hated her. I remember one summer we were back in Illinois visiting with my dad's parents, and we had brought back a videotape of one of my basketball games so they could watch me. The entire video my dad went on and on about how well *she* was doing. He never once mentioned anything about me and how well I was playing. It was kind of embarrassing and hurtful that we hardly ever see my grandparents and they never got to see any of my games, and now when they finally get to, all Dad can talk about is my teammate! Who, truthfully, my grandparents didn't really care about. They cared about watching me play, not some girl they had never met. It really hurt me. I even went to the kitchen and started crying. My mom and grandma had to come into the kitchen to comfort me.

It's been that way about a lot of things, and I never told him what I was thinking and what I was feeling. I always felt like he was comparing me with everyone else. Every other girl was prettier, and smarter, and more athletic. I just always thought that he wanted me to be someone else. Maybe even wanting me to be a boy! He always complains about how I'm not into sports when sports have been a big part of my life! In junior high, I met one of my really good friends through basketball. During freshman year, my best friend started spending time with her sister at school and I could tell she didn't want to hang out with me as much, so I tried to make new friends. I took a leap and tried out for tennis. It was hard at first and I thought about quitting. I didn't know anyone on the first day of tryouts and I felt so out of place, but I met new people and started making new friends. I have met most of my best friends through tennis. I don't know what my life would be like if I hadn't taken that leap and gone out for the tennis team. So for Dad to say that sports don't mean anything to me is just a huge slap in the face! What more does he want? Of course I'm not going to be competing in the Olympics, but I'm pretty athletic for a girl. I've tried a lot of different sports and have done pretty well in all of them, which is more than a lot of people can say.

About the cell phone and iPod issue: Four out of five teenagers have a wireless device. Seventeen million teenagers carry a cell phone! It's just the way it is. Nowadays, a cell phone is a necessity rather than a luxury. Texting is just a way to communicate with people when they aren't right next to you. Of course I would rather have a conversation face-to-face, but the people that you want to talk to aren't always there with you. So texting is a way of being able to be with them and talk to them when you are miles apart. I don't understand why my dad disapproves. He holds a lot of double standards in my opinion. He e-mails constantly. He e-mails his friends. He e-mails his family. He e-mails old co-workers. What's the difference? Texting is e-mailing in a faster way. So instead of having to check the computer 10 times a day, you can just pick up your phone and there it is!

Also, the iPod thing I do not understand. Earlier in the book, he talks about his obsession with music. Music has been a huge part of his life. He loves the lyrics, they connect with him in a way that nothing or nobody else can. He listens to CDs in his car. He has watched the music videos countless numbers of times. He talks about them constantly. So what's wrong when I do the same? What's the difference when I want to listen to my music? Why is it suddenly not okay when I want to go into my little bubble and listen to lyrics that connect with me in a way that nothing and nobody else can? It's just hard for me to grasp the reason he thinks something that means so much to him can't mean as much to me.

Earlier, my dad wrote about how he feels that we don't talk very much and that I don't tell him things like I tell my mom, which is extremely true. I don't tell him lots of things because I know he won't care. Most everything that goes on in my life would seem stupid and petty to him. He doesn't want to know what my friends and I talked about at lunch, he doesn't want to know what the latest information about prom is, he doesn't want to know any of it, so why should I tell him? He thinks that my life is a huge phenomenon where exciting and interesting things happen left and right! But what I find exciting and interesting isn't the same kind of thing he finds exciting and interesting. I will tell him things that really matter, like if one of my friends and I get into a fight or if I have a huge project in a class. But other than that, why does it matter? I already know that what he wants me to say won't be important to him, so why should I say it? I have tried telling him things in the past, but like I said, to him they seem small and insignificant. So then I feel stupid for wasting my time telling him and thinking that it might actually matter to him.

Now that I have stated my side on these issues, I can talk about things that have bothered me through the years.

With Dad, everyone is wrong. He is always right. And even when you prove him wrong, he is still always right. I've learned to just let him have his way, because I already know that no matter how much evidence I have to show that he is wrong, he will still always act like he is right. For example: About a year ago, my friend Emily had spent the night at our house. The next morning we were in my bathroom putting on our makeup and getting ready, and it was getting a little warm so she opened the window. Now with our windows, there are two locks on each side of the frame. To open the window, you have to unlock both of them and push the window up. When the window is up, you don't have to lock it for it to stay up. It will stay up and then when you are ready to close the window, all you have to do is push the window down and lock both sides. Now remember that because it is very important.

So after we got ready, Emily and I left to get job applications from various places, and when we came back, she left to go back home. Later on that day, Dad went into my bathroom and saw the open window, and because there was nobody in the bathroom, he closed it. Well, when he closed it, something happened to the top of the window frame and the two locks broke. He came downstairs furious, saying that Emily and I had broken the window! I was so irritated! The window had been fine when we were up there. It was when he tried to close it that it broke! So I have no idea why he would immediately point fingers at us when it broke while he was touching it.

I texted Emily and told her about what happened and asked her if she had broken the window. She said that she had no idea what I was talking about and that the window had been fine when she had opened it. I asked her to go through the steps that she went through when opening the window. She said she unlocked the two locks, pushed the window up, and then locked the two locks. Right away, I knew what happened! We don't lock the windows when we have them open, and she must have assumed that you had to lock it in order for the window to stay up. And when Dad went to close the window, he must have assumed that the window was still unlocked like it usually is so when he pushed down on it to close it, the locks broke! Nobody was to blame. It was an accident, a misunderstanding. It just frustrated me that Dad would simply assume that it was our fault, when accidentally he was the one who actually broke it. I never told him this, because I knew it wouldn't really matter to him. He would just make up some other excuse like we were being too noisy or messing around too much that we should have noticed that the window had been locked.

It's like that with everything! The TV, the computer, the phone, anything! If it wasn't working right, then it was somebody else's fault. Even if he was the last person to use the TV or the computer, if something was wrong, then it was somebody else's mistake. He was never liable for anything.

Also, Dad's actions and moods have always made it difficult to have friends over at our house. Whenever I want a friend to sleep over or want to have a party for my birthday, I always make sure it's on a night when my dad is working late, usually on a Friday. He does not have a high tolerance for children and loud noise, which I understand, but couldn't he try to be patient sometimes? Or at least act patient? When he gets home from work and I have friends over, he immediately shows that he doesn't want them there. He will complain about us laughing too much or that we are being too loud. And he always has this grimace on his face as if he's in utter pain that we are laughing or having fun. I just feel so sorry and embarrassed for myself and for my friends because I have invited them over for a good time and instead they feel unwelcome.

Through the years, I've felt that my dad has never really loved me. I mean, I knew that he loved me, but it was more of the "you have to love them" kind of love. Like she's your daughter, so you have to love her. It's the first rule in the "Being a Parent" manual: Say you love your child, even if you really don't. Imagine your mom or grandmother telling you your father really does love you and your eyebrows rise up in surprise! That's happened to me—a lot. We all doubt sometimes if our parents really love us, but I have probably doubted more in my 16 years of being that my father has really truly loved me than anyone should in her entire life. I thought that reading his book would make me feel better about everything and would make me see that he really does want me. But to be honest, it hasn't. Reading about how he felt forced into having me and that it was either "have a baby or get a divorce" makes me doubt it even more. I always thought that both my parents wanted me and that they tried for a long time to get pregnant. Now, I know that it was really my mom who wanted me, and that my dad just had me so he wouldn't lose my mom. That says a lot about how much he loved my mom, though. That he would have a baby and go through the horrible steps of being a father just so she wouldn't leave him. It's sweet that he loved her that much. I wish I could say the same for myself, though.

I wish I could have been there to see them in love like that. I do still believe that my parents love each other, but once again it's that feeling that they have to love each other. At least, I feel that way on Dad's part. Second rule: Say you love your wife, even if you really don't. It's hard to tell if he really loves her or if he has just grown so used to being with her that he just thinks it would be too much of a hassle to find someone else. He talks about all these famous female celebrities and practically worships the ground they walk on, when he doesn't do that for my mom. I can't remember the last time I have heard him give her a compliment, and I have never heard him say the words, "You look beautiful." It's hard for me to tell what love is. With seeing my parents, I genuinely cannot tell if it is truly love or if they have just been with each other for so long that they can't picture themselves leaving. Even if the feelings are not really there. If this is a misunderstanding, I hope my parents can clear it up and correct me for my mistakes. But for now, I stand by my assumption of the third rule: Say you love your family, even if you really don't.

Don't get me wrong, Dad has done little things that show he cares, and I will never forget them. That night in seventh grade when I made the "B" team in basketball, he came home from work carrying a pink flower with a small teddy bear wrapped around it. I loved it, and I still keep it on my desk in my room to this day. When I was younger, and he would make my lunch for school, he used to stick little notes in my lunchbox saying things like "I love you" and "I'm proud of you," and I have kept them all. Every single one. I still look at them from time to time, whenever that subtle hint of doubt comes back. I try to believe that those words are true. And I'm pretty sure they are. It's just going to take a while for those years of uncertainty to go away for good.

I think the greatest thing he has ever done that makes me believe he really does love me was when my first boyfriend broke up with me. My (ex) boyfriend said that he didn't love me anymore and that he hadn't had feelings for me in about a month. I was stunned! I had no idea that he felt differently about me. He hadn't acted any differently. Every time we were together, it was exactly the same as when he did have feelings for me. I must give him props, though: He did fake loving someone so perfectly. I'm actually convinced that he never loved me at all, because feelings like that don't go away in a single month.

I was heartbroken. It was literally the toughest thing I have ever had to go through, and I didn't know how Dad would react; if he would be sympathetic or use the old "I told you so" trick. Reaching the assumption that if I can handle the responsibility of being in a relationship, then I should be able to handle the responsibility of when it ended.

However, that was not what happened. The next morning after my ex had dumped me, my dad came into my room and asked me if I was okay. I wasn't. I was trying to be strong, but after he asked me that, I fell apart. I started crying and ran into his arms and told him what had happened. It took me a while to hear over my own loud sobs that he was crying, too. He told me that I was a beautiful girl and that he loved me very much. I knew then that he honestly meant it and that he wasn't saying it because he had to. He wasn't saying it because he was forced to. He wasn't saying it because he was my father and that's what fathers are supposed to say. They were real tears and they were his real words. He knew I was hurting inside and I knew that a little part of him was hurting, too. That's a moment I will never forget for as long as I live.

I hope that this chapter helps his book in some way and helps people to understand better what it's like living with someone with Asperger's syndrome. But truthfully, I didn't write it for the book or for the readers. I didn't even write it for the people suffering from Asperger's. I wrote it so I can finally tell my dad how I really feel. I have never had the guts to tell him how much his words or his actions have hurt me, but now I finally am telling him. And if my theories and statements do not speak the truth, I trust that I will be proven wrong. Hopefully, this weight that I have been carrying with me for years will be lifted.

So, Dad, I just want you to know that I understand now why you have done the things you have done. I understand why you have said the things that you have said. I understand that you did not intend to hurt the people who you have hurt. And I want you to know that I forgive you for everything and that I have and will always, undoubtedly, love you. Fourth rule: Say you love your father, especially if you really do.

CHAPTER TEN: DISCOVERY

In Chapter One, I talked about getting fired from a job I'd had for more than 15 years, but I haven't really talked much about the job itself. For most of the time I worked there, I had a sort of love-hate relationship with the place. I truly loved the job I did, and I know I was quite good at it.

Other things about the job, however, left much to be desired. I only ever made a handful of friends in the entire time I was there. A lot of that is because of me, of course, and my difficulties in dealing with people. I just never knew how to make friends.

In preparing to write this book, I asked some of my former co-workers to share their impressions of me in the workplace. Here's what one of them had to say:

"I always saw Scott around the building or in the production room where he would have to come to copy-edit, which is also where I worked on design and layout. Although quiet, Scott was always very nice and cordial.

"I wasn't the most outgoing girl, so I was never really confident enough to start much of a conversation, especially with another person as quiet as I can be in these situations. I do believe we exchanged smiles and hellos in passing.

"Scott worked there the entire time I did, [that] being over five years . . . and I always thought he was extremely professional and well-liked by his peers."

Another person said:

"I remember Scott as very quiet and hardworking. He always kept to himself at work and at parties. I felt that if I wanted to talk to him, I had to work very hard to draw him into a conversation. . . . It was a lot of work to engage him even in small talk. That, in a nutshell, is how I remember him."

And another:

"I worked with Scott for 13 years, and I had the impression that he was reserved or extremely shy. He was absolutely professional at all times and seemed to have a strong work ethic."

In the years I worked for this company, many times I'd thought about leaving. But something always made me change my mind. My first boss, the one who had invited me out to dinner on my anniversary, was callously fired in 1998. I seriously considered leaving then, but there was no place better to go.

All in all, I must have thought about leaving that job about four or five times. And yet, when I started my 16th year in July of 2006, I felt a strange complacency, like that job was truly what I was meant to do for the rest of my life. At that time, I had no thoughts about leaving. I was content. I tried my best to shut out all the insipid business and personnel decisions that were made and focus solely on my job.

December 2006 was a big turning point in my life. I remember so vividly the day I found out I might have Asperger's syndrome, it's almost like it was yesterday. I was at work, reading a story about autism, when one paragraph really struck a chord with me. In describing the many variations of the autism spectrum, the passage read: "'The spectrum' . . . refers to a range of behaviors, from Asperger's syndrome, a mild version of autism marked by odd tics, a hard time socializing, and, usually, very high intelligence, to the kind of autism you saw in *Rain Man*, where the guy really can't function well at all in the real world."

Until that moment, I had never heard of Asperger's syndrome. But the symptoms mentioned were difficult to ignore. I didn't think I had any odd tics, but I knew I had a hard time socializing, and I was fairly confident that I had high intelligence. So I started to do some research. I looked up Asperger's syndrome on the Internet, and it was like a whole world opened up to me. The more I read about it, the more I was convinced that I had this condition. And the more I realized I had this condition, the more certain things about my behavior—and my life—started to make sense.

At the time, my wife and I had been seeing a counselor to work on some issues in our marriage. This counselor suggested that I open up a bit, try to make more friends. I knew I had problems with social situations, and I knew that my depression had sometimes made me a difficult person to live with. And I had been through counseling before, so I pretty much knew what to expect. Never, in all my years of counseling, did anyone mention that I might have Asperger's, or some similar mental disorder.

After reading more about Asperger's, the first thing I did was to tell my wife. I had printed out a description of Asperger's symptoms from a Web site and showed it to her. After reading it, she simply said, "That would explain a lot."

The next thing I did was to call my counselor. After reading her a list of the symptoms, she was certain I was onto something. She told me I should see a psychiatrist and get a diagnosis. Unfortunately, this was just a couple of weeks before Christmas 2006, and every psychiatrist I called was booked until the middle of January. I made an appointment for the earliest date in January that I could get and began an agonizing waiting process.

My next idea, I thought, was a stroke of genius. I knew I had very few friends at work and often had difficulty interacting with my co-workers. I suspected that my Asperger's was hindering my social behavior at work. My idea was to send out an e-mail to all the members of my department, describing Asperger's syndrome in detail, and making it clear that I believed that this condition was the reason for my seeming distant, or aloof, or however my co-workers saw me. Because I had a hard time dealing with people one-on-one, I figured that sending out a mass e-mail was the best way to accomplish this goal. I had already told my supervisor that I thought I had Asperger's, and her response was rather cold. But before I sent out the e-mail, I figured I should run the idea past her to make sure it was okay. Her reply to me, in an e-mail, absolutely astounded me. Her response was twofold: Not only was I not to send out my e-mail, but I was never to bring up the subject of Asperger's syndrome again. I was so floored by her reaction that I kept the e-mail, in case I needed to use it in my defense in the future.

My supervisor's main concern seemed to be about the Health Insurance Portability and Accountability Act (HIPAA), which ensures an employee's privacy regarding medical conditions. The problem with that logic is, even though my supervisor was forbidden by law to discuss my condition, I could tell whoever I wanted.

Dealing with my supervisor's puzzling behavior added to what was already another stressful time for me personally. Not only had I just discovered that I may have an autistic disorder, but my 99-year-old great-grandmother had died December 6, 2006, just 42 days short of her 100th birthday. Even though my great-grandmother was in poor health and lived in a nursing home, my family had been planning a 100th-birthday celebration for her for some time. The entire family was saddened by her passing, and it was difficult for me to deal with the loss emotionally. But I was in no way prepared for what was to happen next.

CHAPTER ELEVEN: TERMINATION

It was shortly after 3 p.m. on Tuesday, January 16, 2007. I was called into my supervisor's office for what was seemingly a routine face-to-face meeting. After working with the same company for 15 and a half years, what else would I have expected? But this was not to be an ordinary meeting. As I entered my supervisor's office, I noticed that the woman who was the head of the Human Resources department was also there.

I sat down facing my supervisor, and he began thusly: "There's been another complaint about you," he said. My mouth dropped open, and I had no idea of what to say. During the previous six months, two women had accused me of sexual harassment. Each time, I could not believe what I was hearing, as I didn't think I had done anything to warrant such complaints.

In the summer of 2006, my wife and daughter and I had begun counseling, and our analyst had tried to get me to open up a bit, to try to make new friends. And that was pretty much what I was attempting to do. I knew the women who had made the complaints against me, but from my point of view, I was just trying to start conversations with them, trying to make friends. Socially awkward? Most likely. Harassing? Definitely not. At least that was the way I saw it. I had tried to make friends with men as well, with some success. But men weren't likely to accuse me of harassing them.

The first complaint supposedly came from a woman who I had known for a short period of time. I didn't know her that well, but one day we passed each other in the hallway, and she gave me a nice compliment. Because I didn't have many friends at work, I couldn't remember the last time someone gave me a compliment. By the time I got back to my desk, I was practically giddy. I decided to send her an e-mail telling her that her compliment had made my whole day. And it was the truth. It did make me quite happy.

During the next couple of weeks, I sent her a few more e-mails, all of them innocuous in nature. I asked her how her day was going, if she might ever want to go out to lunch, that sort of thing. Again, I felt I was just trying to make a friend—I meant nothing sexual or out of line. So it came as quite a shock when my supervisor told me there was a complaint about me. Because it was the first complaint, my supervisor said there would be no disciplinary action taken, just a talk. I stopped e-mailing the woman immediately and could not figure out why she would complain about anything I had done.

About three months went by, and in late November of 2006, I was told to report to the HR office. I was informed that there had been another complaint. My supervisor accompanied me to the HR office, but the woman who had made the complaint was not there.

This second complaint came from even farther out of left field than the first one. The woman who had made the complaint worked in the production department of the publication where I was employed. I remember having perhaps three conversations with her, ever. The head of the HR department read off a list of complaints that the woman from production had made against me.

I was flabbergasted. Among the complaints were that I had complimented my co-worker on something she was wearing (a conversation starter, I figured) and that I hung around the production room more than she thought I should have. For one thing, the printer was in the production room, and it just happened to be near this woman's desk. I had to go to production frequently to pick up pages off the printer and to discuss work-related matters—necessary to doing my job and something I had done for 15 years without incident. I was never there longer than I had to be.

There were a couple of other allegations from the second complainant, but for each one, I had a simple and logical explanation. At least, it seemed simple and logical to me. I was distraught about being accused of harassment, especially by a co-worker who hadn't been there long and who I didn't know well. After the meeting, I thought everything had been cleared up. I explained my side of the story and went back to my business. Before I left the HR office, however, I was cautioned that this had been the second complaint against me. If there was another one, it might cost me my job.

I was extremely upset after that meeting. I felt I had done nothing wrong, certainly nothing that would have warranted a harassment complaint. The meeting with HR happened at the end of the day, before I was ready to go home. On the way home, the meeting was all I could think about. Of course, driving home, I thought of many more things that I could have and possibly should have said at the meeting. Like, for instance, why had the woman who filed the complaint never said anything directly to me? Why wasn't she present at the meeting in the HR office? In fact, that was to be a pattern with all of the women who made complaints against me. None of them ever said a word to me to let me know that I was doing something that upset them or bothered them in some way. If they had had the courtesy to let me know something was wrong, I would have apologized, said it would never happen again, and that would have been the end of it.

Another thing I thought about while driving home was that I should have asked to see the complaint against me. The HR boss merely read off a list of complaints from this woman, and I gave my responses verbally. If I had been able to see a written document, I would have responded to each complaint in writing, and then my side of the story would have been on the record as well. I've always been better at forming my thoughts in writing, and I'm uncomfortable at speaking if I'm put under pressure. Needless to say, the HR meeting was a high-pressure situation, and I probably didn't come off too well.

Back in my supervisor's office in January of 2007, after my boss told me that there had been a third complaint, my thoughts wandered wildly. I had tried to be on my best behavior, keeping to myself as much as possible. Luckily, I was an expert at maintaining distance. I had no idea of the origin of this latest complaint. All the while, my supervisor kept talking, but I barely heard him. But when he said, "I'm going to have to terminate you," my full attention was brought back.

I couldn't believe this was happening. I had been a loyal, responsible, hardworking employee of this company for 15 and a half years. I had received three complaints of sexual harassment in a span of six months. As with the previous meeting in the HR office, I found the words to explain myself hard to come by. I knew in my heart that I had not harassed anyone, intentionally.

The third complaint was as bewildering as the first two. Apparently, according to one complaint, this female co-worker didn't like the way I "looked" at her. What does that mean? I wasn't aware that I had "looked" at her in any certain way. In fact, I never knew that anything I had said or done had bothered her. But again, as in the previous instances, the woman who made the complaint never said a word to me personally. Nor was she present in the office when the latest complaint was brought to my attention. And this last time, I was not even given a chance to defend myself. I was fired from my job, and that was that.

Later, many questions came to mind. I was doubly distressed not to have thought of them at the time of termination. Among them, did the company really believe that I would all of a sudden start harassing women after 15 years? It just didn't make sense, at least not to me. Maybe the higher-ups in the company, having to save face, had their own ideas. All I know is, if I had been able to explain myself, everything could have been resolved quickly and easily.

Of course, I knew the reason behind my awkward social behavior that may have contributed to the complaints against me. It was Asperger's syndrome, a condition that I had only just discovered a little more than a month before losing my job. If I had been able to state my side of the story this last time, I would have listed my disorder as the main reason for the complaints.

Unfortunately, the first two complaints came before I had found out that I had Asperger's. The thing that really bothers me, even after all this time, is that I believe it mostly came down to a series of misunderstandings. If my co-workers had been made to understand my disorder and how it affected me socially—and if my supervisors had taken my condition seriously in the first place—everything that led to my being fired could have been resolved rather easily.

My termination affected me deeply. After all, it wasn't just a job. I was attached to that place. And I was always dedicated to doing my job, even when I wasn't treated well by co-workers or supervisors. Now, all of a sudden, that job was taken from me.

To say that it was a trying period for me is an understatement.

CHAPTER TWELVE:
AFTERMATH

The early part of 2007 was truly difficult for me. Trying to cope with a newfound mental disorder while having to look for a new job posed quite a challenge. In the days after I was fired, I called several lawyers to find out if I had a basis for a discrimination lawsuit. Firing someone with a mental disorder had to be illegal, I figured. I had told both of my immediate supervisors about my condition, but they appeared to do nothing. If I could prove that I had told my supervisors, and the company had fired me anyway, I thought that would be in violation of the Americans with Disabilities Act.

The lawyers were helpful, but in the end, they said winning a lawsuit was a long shot. First of all, I only suspected I had Asperger's syndrome. I hadn't had it officially diagnosed yet. And of course, there were the three sexual-harassment complaints against me. One lawyer said if I had had a medical diagnosis, a lawsuit might have a chance. But without a diagnosis, there wasn't much I could do.

The first order of business was to get my condition properly diagnosed. My appointment with the psychiatrist in January 2007 didn't go exactly as I had planned. I had printed all the information about Asperger's that I could find from the Internet, and I had taken a few online tests to see if I had the disorder, which I had also printed out. I was well-prepared for my visit with the psychiatrist. However, at the conclusion of the first session, the doctor said he needed more information to determine if I had Asperger's. He was fairly certain that I had social anxiety disorder but wasn't sure about Asperger's. I had two more sessions with him, with little progress. Finally, the doctor referred me to a psychologist who had the office next door.

I took a more immediate liking to that psychologist. Before my first session, he had me take a test of about 600 questions to determine my mental makeup. After the test, I sat down in his office and we talked. It turned out that the psychologist had a son who had Asperger's, so he was better able to recognize the signs. He made several comments about me, about some nervous habits he observed while I was in his office. He told me I had "intense" eyes. I wasn't sure what that meant, but maybe it would explain the third woman's complaint about the way I "looked" at her. The first visit with the psychologist went well.

I saw the psychologist two more times in the next couple of weeks. At the end of the third visit, he determined that I did, indeed, have Asperger's. So I finally got the diagnosis I needed in March 2007—a mere two months after I was fired.

In the meantime, I had gotten a job with another newspaper chain that produced 14 community papers around the state, and I met some new people who I liked very much. Things seemed to be going rather well. But as luck would have it, in July of 2007 financial problems forced the company to close five of its 14 Arizona papers. There would be no layoffs, per se, but I was moved from the editorial department into sales. It didn't take a genius to realize that Asperger's syndrome and sales don't mix, so I began looking for yet another job. Fortunately, I landed my current position with a daily newspaper.

I'd like to relate an interesting anecdote, something that happened while I was at the community paper, that really illustrates, I think, how bizarre the situation was at the company where I was terminated. Because I had been fired for allegedly sexually harassing women at work, I was paralyzed with fear when I started my new job as far as what I should or should not say around women. I was painfully reserved, usually never saying more than was required of me.

Then one day our office secretary, who happened to be female, asked me to do her a favor. In our office, there was a collection of files of businesses that had advertised with the newspaper in the past but did not currently advertise. Every once in a while, employees would go through the files and cold-call the businesses to see if they were interested in advertising once again. Around the office, these files were known as "tickler" files.

One day the office secretary asked me to put a folder into the tickler file. I responded, "Is that near the French tickler file?" It was just a spontaneous comment, but even that got me to wondering if it would be considered harassment.

About a week later, some of the employees went out to lunch together. I and a few others rode with the office secretary to and from the restaurant.

On the way back, the office secretary made a point to tell me how glad she was that I had made the French tickler comment the week before. She said, "I always thought you were such a prude. You were always so quiet. After you said that, I felt like I could loosen up around you a little more."

Although I was glad to know that no offense was taken, I also felt like I couldn't win no matter what I did. Being cautious and reserved wasn't the appropriate way to act at work, either.

It's situations like these that have me frustrated with life in general. I was never good around people even before I knew about Asperger's. Now that I know about it, and continue to deal with it, I'm just as lost as I was before in dealing with people. It's something I'll probably struggle with for the rest of my life.

I wish I could say this book has a happy ending, but I'm not sure if it does. Yes, I've had some setbacks in life, as everyone does, but I also have had some precious and happy moments. Obviously, my wedding and the birth of my daughter were highlights. I've met my favorite singer, Sarah McLachlan, on three separate occasions. I've met some of my other favorite singers, too: Melissa Etheridge twice; Natalie Merchant once; Anna Nalick once; and Margo Timmins, the lead singer of Cowboy Junkies, twice. I've seen my two favorite baseball teams, the Arizona Diamondbacks and Chicago White Sox, win World Series titles. I even went to one of the Diamondbacks' World Series games. A friend and I once climbed to the top of the "Hollywood" sign in California. These are memories I will treasure forever.

But I still get sad, and I still get depressed every now and then. Maybe that's just life. Regarding my depression, I'd say it's gotten better. Recently I discovered another drug that I've added to my daily mixture—Abilify, which is supposed to be taken in conjunction with other antidepressants. I had some trouble adjusting to it in the beginning, but now it seems like it has made me feel better overall. But I can't see myself going off antidepressants anytime soon.

As for my Asperger's condition, I've only known about it for a relatively short time, so I'm still adjusting to it and learning about it. I've also been trying to make others aware of the disorder so that they may come to understand people like me. Those who don't have Asperger's may not understand what it's like to have it, but understanding is the key. No matter how hard it is for "normal" people to understand me, it is 10 times more difficult for me to understand them. I'm not looking for pity, and I don't need anyone's sympathy. I just need people to understand why I act the way I do at times, and to accept me the way I am. If this book can make a few people understand this disorder, and possibly recognize it either in themselves or someone they know, then it will have served its purpose.

EPILOGUE:
CLOSURE, POSSIBLY?

Throughout this book, I've included observations from family, friends and co-workers in an attempt to help readers as well as myself understand how someone with Asperger's comes across to others. In preparing to write the book, I contacted as many people as possible. Two of them, former co-workers, were music writers for the newspaper I had worked for, and both mentioned my fondness for Sarah McLachlan:

"I never had the opportunity to work with Scott too much, but [knowing about Asperger's syndrome] makes me understand his distance, but more so his love for Sarah McLachlan. I knew then, when we were both at Lilith Fair [in 1998], I had a great girlfriend who was dying to see the acts while I didn't care that much, but I could see Scott's enthusiasm, how endeared he was to the acts. I'm sorry that we didn't break whatever barriers back then so we could have been better friends."

And this:

"It was always clear to me that Scott was very bright and very knowledgeable about a wide range of subjects. On some level, though, I found him sort of impenetrable. I'm pretty shy myself, so I'm not generally very comfortable opening up with new people, and I sensed shyness in Scott as well, but it also felt like something more. It was a distance, a sense that he was vaguely unapproachable. I sensed, maybe wrongly, that he thought of us (the writers) as kind of stupid and annoying, even though he never said that.

"Another thing that stands out, because it was a rare case of Scott approaching me about a non-work issue, was when he asked me if I could get him backstage to meet Sarah McLachlan. I wasn't able to help with that, but, as I recall, he met her at a radio-station interview. I knew that for Scott to ask for a favor like that, it had to be very important to him. I was intrigued by that."

It disappointed me when I read that this person thought that I believed the writers to be stupid and annoying, because that was never the case. I always had great respect for the writers. And if this is how I was perceived by some of my co-workers, then I am very sorry for that.

Reading the positive recollections from friends gives me a good, warm feeling. It makes me feel like I really have touched people in my life.

However, in the spirit of fairness, writing this book also meant trying to get in touch with the women who had filed sexual-harassment complaints against me, to get their take about what transpired. It was a thorny issue, though. How would I reach them? If I were to just write to them, out of the blue, maybe they would consider that harassment as well.

I had written a couple of letters to the company that fired me, asking for written documentation of all the "complaints" against me. What I got in return was a snippy letter from a lawyer that said, in part, "your conduct, notwithstanding your post termination denials or excuses, made it untenable for your employment at the company to continue," but never once mentioned my Asperger's syndrome. Maybe the bit about "post termination denials" helps the lawyer sleep better, but it certainly didn't help my situation at all.

Finally, it was Facebook that provided the answer. All three of the women who had filed complaints against me had Facebook profiles. So I took a chance and sent a message to all three of them. I tried to come up with something as harmless as I could, something that would let them know I wanted to talk to them, but without being confrontational in any way.

The first woman who replied was a joy to talk with. She had always been a pleasant person, and the harassment complaint, the first one against me, came out of nowhere, as far as I was concerned. I always wondered what I had done to warrant a complaint. Here is her side of the story:

"In all honesty I *did not* complain that you harassed me. I vaguely remember being brought in to [the business manager's] office and asked about e-mail exchanges but I never instigated or pursued anything of the sort.

"I am sorry for your struggles and am also sorry that I was pulled in to the mix. I certainly would not go out of my way to cost a person their job."

Because the series of e-mails I had sent her was what had sparked her complaint, I asked her about them.

"To be completely honest, I don't remember the e-mails. So to me, that suggests that there wasn't anything remotely offensive."

She had moved to Los Angeles and was not involved in the publishing field anymore, but I asked her what she remembered about me, if anything.

"I remember that you did come off very shy but it wasn't in an unusual way. It was almost like you felt unworthy. . . . Does that make sense? It's not one of those things that is comfortable to come out and say, but had you told one person [about Asperger's] and it had become whispered conversation amongst the hallways, I do believe it would have changed the way people interacted with you. Inspired almost a challenge amongst people . . . to make you feel comfortable around them. More hellos in the hallways, etc. People are weird like that.

"I look forward to your book and hope it brings you a lot of success! This seems to have affected you in quite a way . . . imagine the people you could help. That is a very noble accomplishment."

We ended up e-mailing back and forth for quite a while. She was very nice to talk to, just as I had remembered her being when I worked with her. I guess the saying is true, that time heals all wounds.

Unfortunately, I did not have the same luck contacting the other two women who complained about me. They both blocked any future e-mails from me. It would have been nice to get a contribution from those two women, but I have to respect that they may have their own reasons for not wanting to participate.

Obviously, social relationships have been a lifelong challenge for me, and I'm sure they'll continue to be so. But I'm lucky to have many friends and co-workers—many of whom are quoted in this book—who have been willing to accept me for who I am. I'm even luckier to have a beautiful, patient wife and daughter who have stood by me through tough times and helped me come to grips with my condition. Asperger's sufferers may find it difficult to build meaningful relationships, but as my case clearly demonstrates, it's not impossible.

I don't know how many people in this world have Asperger's syndrome. It may manifest itself differently in those who have it, and no two people with Asperger's may behave the same way or have the same symptoms. For those reading this, there may be people in your own lives with Asperger's and you don't even know it. For that matter, they may not even know it. I didn't know about my condition until I was 44 years old. Even though it's now being diagnosed in young children, there are probably many people who have Asperger's, or perhaps some other mild form of autism, and not even know it.

This book is meant to educate people who don't know about the disorder, and comfort those who have it so they don't feel alone. I hope it has done that.